ASSIGNMENTS
BUSINESS STUDIES

Stephen Danks

Lynne Cross

Stephen Danks
B.Sc. (Hons), Dip. Marketing, Cert. Ed.,
Vice Principal, Bolton Metropolitan College

Lynne Cross
B.Ed., Dip. Educational Management, Cert.Ed.,
Lecturer in Business Studies, Macclesfield College;
GCSE Business Studies Examiner

Nelson

Thomas Nelson and Sons Ltd
Nelson House Mayfield Road
Walton-on-Thames Surrey
KT12 5PL UK

51 York Place
Edinburgh
EH1 3JD UK

Thomas Nelson (Hong Kong) Ltd
Toppan Building 10/F
22A Westlands Road
Quarry Bay Hong Kong

Distributed in Australia by

Thomas Nelson Australia
480 La Trobe Street
Melbourne Victoria 3000
and in Sydney, Brisbane, Adelaide and Perth

© Stephen Danks and Lynne Cross 1989
First Published by Thomas Nelson and Sons Ltd 1989

ISBN 0-17-448114-4

NPN 9 8 7 6 5 4 3 2 1

Printed and Bound in the U.K. by Bell and Bain Ltd,
Glasgow

Contents

Preface   5
Notes for students   6
Introduction: The development of economic activity   7

Background to business: Assignments 1–6

1 The division of labour   9
Specialisation ● Mass production: advantages and
disadvantages

2 Population trends   11
Census ● Birth rates ● Death rates ● Migration ●
Age ● Geographical and occupational distribution ●
Working population

3 International trade   14
Reasons for trade ● Imports ● Exports ● Balance of
Payments ● Barriers to trade ● Government influence

4 European Community   17
Member countries ● Aims of EC policy ● Effect on UK:
consumers and businesses

5 Something to bank on   19
Functions of banks ● Types of bank account ● Cheques ●
Post Office Girobank ● Building societies

6 Cashless society   23
Methods of payment ● Credit cards ● Automated banking

Multiple choice 1   26

Business structure and organisation: Assignments 7–13

7 Who owns the business?   29
Sole traders ● Partnerships ● Private and public limited
companies ● Co-operatives ● Franchising ● Public
ownership

8 A local business study   31
Business objectives ● Location and organisation ●
Importance to local community

9 Shopping around   34
Chain of distribution ● Wholesalers ● Types of retail
outlets ● Retailing without shops

10 Which site would you choose?   37
Location ● Analysis of potential sites ● Government
influence ● Competition

11 Scale of production   40
Economies of scale ● Size and growth of firms ●
Integration ● Survival of small firms

12 Business finance   43
Sources of capital ● Stock Exchange ● Why share prices
fluctuate

13 It's a risky business   45
Insurance ● Premiums and risks ● Documents ● Principles
● Business insurance ● Uninsurable risks

Multiple choice 2   48

Business behaviour: Assignments 14–20

14 Market research survey   51
Market research ● Desk and field research ● Sampling ●
Interviewing ● Marketing mix

15 Cadbury's Dairy Milk   53
Marketing ● Product life cycle ● Product planning ●
Terminology

16 Why advertise?   55
Methods of sales promotion ● Advertising ● Advertising
media ● Control of advertising

17 You want it when?   59
Importance of transport ● Choice ● Types ● Containers ●
Future developments ● Distribution problems

18 Business documents   63
Documents used in a business transaction ● Value Added
Tax ● Trade and cash discount ● Calculating an order

19 Murphy's break-even   65
Fixed and variable costs ● Average costs ● Break-even

20 Ritetime's final accounts   67
Gross and net profit ● Assets and liabilities ● Balance
sheet ● Working capital ● Simple ratios

Multiple choice 3   70

People in business: Assignments 21–24

21 Jackie Hunter's promotion   73
Motivation ● Job satisfaction ● Personnel problems

22 Dispute at Bennett's   76
Industrial relations ● Trade unions ● Collective
bargaining ● Industrial action ● Reasons for disputes ●
ACAS

23 Payslip   80
Wages and salaries ● Voluntary and statutory deductions ●
Calculating wage payments ● Fringe benefits ● Gross and
net pay

24 Getting the message   82
Need for effective communication ● Methods of
communication ● Importance of new technology

Multiple choice 4   84

31973

Government influence on business activity:
Assignments 25–30

25 Pitstop   87

Social costs and benefits ● Profit motive ● Government control

26 Sunday trading   91

Government legislation ● Arguments for/against Sunday trading ● Pressure groups

27 Where are the jobs?   94

Regional problems ● Assisted areas ● Government measures

28 The Budget   97

Taxation ● The Budget ● Public expenditure

29 Safe and happy at work?   99

Working conditions ● Health and safety ● Effects on morale and efficiency

30 But it's faulty   102

Need for consumer protection ● Government legislation ● Consumer bodies and organisations ● Labelling and standards ● Professional and trade associations ● Codes of practice

Multiple choice 5   106

Revision: Assignments 31–32

31 Sharon and Tracy in business ● Issues associated with starting a business   109

32 Let's revise ● Crossword   111

Glossary of business terms   112
List of useful addresses   115
Index   117
Acknowledgements   119

Preface

This is not a conventional text. It has been specially written to provide a programme of practical student-based activities to meet the National Criteria for GCSE Business Studies. **Assignments in Business Studies** is also suitable for selective use on other courses, including GCSE Business and Information Studies, GCSE Commerce, GCSE Economics, BTEC Business Studies, TVEI, CPVE and other introductory courses such as RSA and Pitman.

The coursework element of GCSE requires a new approach to teaching so as to develop students' practical knowledge and understanding of the subject: GCSE examinations also test skills in numeracy, literacy, investigation, selection and interpretation of relevant information. Based on current business practice and organisation, this text has been written to meet these needs. It uses activity-based assignments to involve students throughout the learning process. This book can be used on its own or in conjunction with an introductory text.

The core of **Assignments in Business Studies** is 32 assignments, introduced by helpful notes for students on obtaining information and on the the presentation of their work. There are 100 multiple choice questions with detachable answers, – should the teacher wish to remove them – a list of useful addresses, a glossary of business terms and an index. A teacher's book with suggested answers for each assignment, together with notes for guidance, is also available.

The assignments feature a variety of practical activities, suitable for mixed abilities, including role play, data response, problem solving, case studies, surveys and visits. Assignments are clearly structured and comprise:

- a section of explanatory background information
- several tasks designed to give practice in a variety of skills and enable all students to demonstrate positive achievement
- lively and interesting illustrations
- opportunities for individual and group visits both inside and outside the classroom
- coursework material suitable for learning and/or assessment purposes
- ideas for further development

The book is intended mainly as a class text but can be used equally well by individual students who wish to develop their studies. This is particularly important given the current growth of self-study learning.

The authors welcome, via the publishers, any comments, favourable or otherwise, on the book. Such feedback will enable subsequent editions to be amended, if necessary, and made even more useful to students and teachers alike.

Stephen Danks
Lynne Cross
1989

Note: For reasons of textual fluency you will find the words 'he' or 'she' have sometimes been used in the book. However, in most cases, the person referred to could be of either sex.

Notes for students

You will find that this book contains several different types of assignments including role plays, case studies, projects and practical exercises. These are designed to encourage you to take an active part in the process of learning.

A number of the activities require you to work outside the classroom either as an individual or as a member of a group. Some assignments will also require you to make oral presentations.

Obtaining information

In some of the assignments you will be asked to make use of a library or other sources of information. A glossary of business terms has been included to help you to understand any terms and concepts not explained in the text.

You will also be asked to contact various organisations to obtain information. A list of useful addresses is given on page 115. An example of the type of letter which you might write is given below. You could use either your school or home address and you should keep copies of any letters for inclusion in your coursework folder.

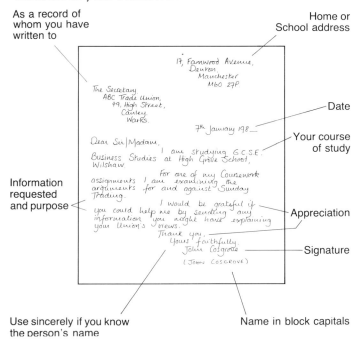

As a record of whom you have written to

Home or School address

Date

Your course of study

Information requested and purpose

Appreciation

Signature

Use sincerely if you know the person's name

Name in block capitals

Assessment

Most assignments carry a total of 50 marks, the breakdown of which is indicated in the text. Several assignments are research projects where marks are allocated for research, analysis of the information obtained, evaluation and presentation.

Presentation

It is important that your work is well organised and neatly presented. Research assignments contain guidance on layout and presentation: graphs, pie charts, pictographs and bar charts are particularly good methods of presenting any numerical information.

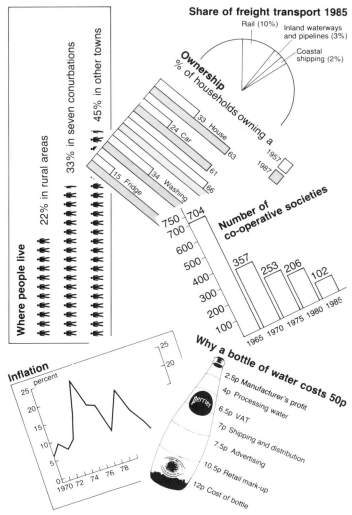

Examples of some methods of presenting information

It is important that you always read the background information and assignment material carefully before starting the tasks. You will find that this will help you by increasing your understanding of what you have to do and will improve the quality of your work. Finally, remember it is important that all written work is presented in your own words.

We hope that you will enjoy using this text and be successful in your coursework and examinations.

Introduction: the development of economic activity

Barter

There were no shops in primitive societies. The simple needs of people for food, clothing and shelter were satisfied from what they could grow, hunt or make for themselves, that is, they were **self-sufficient**. Later, people began to specialise in producing just one or a few items which they were particularly good at making. This **division of labour** enabled people to produce more than they needed for themselves. This led to the development of **trade** as they exchanged their surplus for other goods.

This earliest form of trade was called **barter**. As specialisation increased, **money** was introduced to make the process of exchange easier. This led to an increase in the quantity of goods produced and the rapid development of trade both at home and overseas.

In order to produce goods and services, four essential resources: land, labour, capital and enterprise are needed. These are called **factors of production**. A country's total production will depend on the quality and quantity of these resources.

As the diagram shows, **production** can be classified as **primary**, **secondary** or **tertiary**. The growth of production and trade depends upon a number of important services including banking, insurance, transport, wholesaling and communications. You will also notice that there are many direct (personal) services which are not part of the process of trade but help to increase production by looking after people's general health and welfare.

It is this brief outline of economic activity which provides the framework for the assignments in this text.

Money

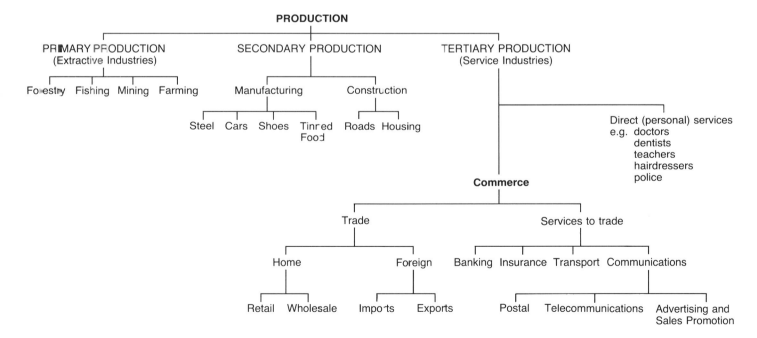

The three types of production – primary, secondary, tertiary

Background to business

Assignment 1

Introduction

Assignment 1 is a role-play exercise based on the division of labour. Working in small groups it will give practical experience of the method of production which is used in most industries today.

On completion of this assignment you should be able to:

1 explain the concept of the division of labour;
2 appreciate how it is used in industry;
3 describe both the advantages and disadvantages of such a system.

Background information

Nowadays it is common for people to specialise in doing particular jobs, for example, people work as farmers, electricians, engineers and teachers. Even within the same occupation people specialise in performing certain types of work; there are, for example, electrical engineers, mechanical engineers and civil engineers.

Examples of specialisation

The division of labour

This **division of labour** is now widely used in modern industry. Work is divided into a number of processes along a 'production' or 'assembly line' with each worker specialising in carrying out just one or two tasks. Car factories, for example, are organised in this way. The shell of a car begins at one end of the 'line'. It then moves along a conveyor belt system where different parts of the vehicle are added by each worker.

Some of the stages in the production of a car using an assembly line

A modern production line

The division of labour has both advantages and disadvantages.

Advantages

- It enables **mass production** to take place. Goods can be produced in large quantities which reduces unit costs.
- **Specialised machinery and equipment** can be used.
- **Practice makes perfect**   Each person becomes faster and better at his or her job.
- **Quicker training**   Training is quicker because jobs are easier to learn.
- **Specialisation**   Workers can specialise in what they can do best.

Disadvantages

- **Boredom**   Workers are always repeating the same task.
- **Standardisation**   Products need to be standardised for mass production to take place, that is, large quantities of virtually identical products are made and this may limit individual choice. Consider, for example, the standardisation of the clothing which people wear.
- **Dependence on others**   For example, absent or slow workers could disrupt the production line.
- **Decline in crafts and skills**   Goods are made by machine instead of by hand.

However, mass production of goods is not suitable unless there is a large market in which to sell them, for example, there would be no point in mass producing ships, aeroplanes or racing cars. On the other hand, pens, chocolates, toothpaste, light bulbs, television sets and family cars are bought by a great many people and all have **mass markets** and therefore can be produced on a large scale. Thus the extent of division of labour is limited by the size of the market.

Assignment

You are asked to carry out an exercise based on the assembly of a product. It will enable you to experience for yourself how the division of labour operates.

On this production line, goods are being assembled by hand

You will need to choose a product which can be assembled by a team of 'workers'. Four suggestions of products which can be easily obtained are:

- **coloured chalks** An assortment of colours could be collected and packed into boxes.
- **sweets** Sweets could be wrapped, sorted and packed into boxes.
- **paper** A teaching handout, magazine or other papers could be collated and stapled together.
- **ball-point pens** There should be at least three parts in the most basic pen which, when assembled, could be boxed to make a fourth process.

Tasks

1 At least two teams (A and B) are needed, each consisting of four or five 'workers' plus timekeeper(s) and checker(s). Each team will need to prepare the chosen product and then assemble it using the procedure below.
   a Each individual in team A assembles the chosen product by themselves. This exercise is repeated several times until an agreed target of, say, 25 assembled products is achieved.
   b At the same time, team B is organised into an 'assembly line' using the division of labour. This group also assembles 25 products.
   c The timekeepers will keep a record of how long each group takes to achieve the agreed target.
   d The checkers are needed to ensure that each product has been correctly assembled. Any 'faulty' work must be noted.
2 You should now take part in a class discussion on the exercise.
3 In your own words write a brief note of your observations on the exercise under the following headings.
   a My definition of the division of labour. (2)
   b The advantages and disadvantages of using the division of labour. (10)
   c The division of labour in my school/college. Use a diagram if this helps. (15)
   d Five examples of the division of labour in the area where I live. (5)
   e The main ways in which I would be affected if mass production did not exist today. (8)

Further development

The following ideas could be used to develop this assignment:

1 If time permits, the two teams could reverse roles and repeat the exercise.
2 Additional assembly processes could be added, for example, sticking on prices or stock codes.
3 Arrange a visit to a local factory to see an assembly line in operation.
4 Discuss how the factors of production relate to the division of labour.

Assignment 2

Introduction

Assignment 2 is a detailed study of the UK's population. It consists of a range of statistical data from which you are asked to identify current population trends. It can be undertaken as an individual or group activity.

On completion of this assignment you should be able to:

1 identify key information from data;
2 define a variety of population terms;
3 explain why people are now living longer;
4 describe the present age and occupational distribution of the population.

Background information

The population of a country can only be accurately found by taking a **census**, that is, by counting it. In the UK this takes place every ten years when all households are required to give information about the type of property in which they live and the people who live in it. This includes details of their age, sex and occupation. The information obtained is used by the government for future planning.

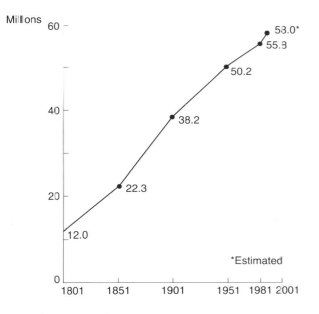

UK population growth 1801–2001

As the diagram shows, the UK's population grew rapidly in the 19th century but has grown more slowly since. Changes in the size of the population are affected by changes in the birth rate, death rate and by migration.

Population trends

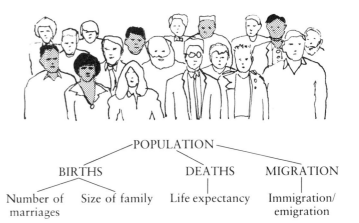

POPULATION
BIRTHS — DEATHS — MIGRATION
Number of   Size of family   Life expectancy   Immigration/
marriages   emigration

Factors affecting the size of a population

In the UK, **death rates** have fallen considerably in the 20th century due largely to improved medical knowledge and better food, housing, clothing, sanitation and working conditions. People now have a much longer life expectancy than in the past. **Birth rates** have also fallen due to improved methods of birth control, lower infant mortality (that is fewer children dying in infancy), more working women and couples preferring alternatives such as cars and foreign holidays to spending money on children.

UK Birth and Death rates (per thousand of the population)		
Year	Birth rate	Death rate
1851	35.5	22.7
1901	28.7	17.3
1951	15.5	11.9
1987	13.3	11.9

(Source: *Annual Abstract of Statistics/Social Trends*)

When people come to live in the UK they are known as **immigrants**. People who move from the UK to other countries are called **emigrants**. The difference between the number who leave and the number who enter the country to live is called **net migration**. Traditionally, the UK has had a net loss of population through migration.

Age distribution refers to the number of people of different ages in the population. It is important because it affects the size of the labour force, the demand for goods and services and the types of houses, schools and other facilities required. The present overall pattern in the UK is that of an ageing population, that is, there is an increasing proportion of people over the age of 65.

The **geographical distribution** of the population shows two main trends. First, some 30 per cent of the population live in the seven largest conurbations: Greater London, West Midlands, Greater Manchester, Central Clydeside, West Yorkshire, Merseyside and Tyneside. Secondly, a movement from Northern Ireland, Scotland and the North where unemployment is high, to the South and Midlands where job prospects, housing and other facilities are generally better.

The **working population** is the number of people in work or available for work. It consists of everyone with a job, those registered as unemployed and the self-employed. The working population has increased since the Second World War as more women seek paid employment, and is now approximately 28 million of which 16 million are men.

The number of people employed in different jobs is referred to as the **occupational distribution**. These occupations can be classified under three main headings:

- **Primary** agriculture, forestry, fishing, mining and quarrying;
- **Secondary** manufacturing and construction;
- **Tertiary (services)** distribution, transport, financial services, catering and hotels, and national and local government.

Assignment

Having read the background information, study the following population data and complete the tasks that follow.

Tasks

Tasks 1 and 2 are based on the table below.

	Life Expectancy in the UK 1901–1981							
	1901	1911	1921	1931	1951	1961	1971	1981
Men	48	52	56	58	66	68	69	70
Women	52	55	59	62	71	74	75	76

1 a What is the name given to the survey of population which took place in each of the above years? *(1)*
  b What type of information does it contain? *(2)*
  c Why do you think that a survey did not take place in 1941? *(1)*
2 a Explain the term 'life expectancy'. *(1)*
  b Identify two main trends from the above data. *(2)*

Tasks 3 and 4 are based on the following pie charts.

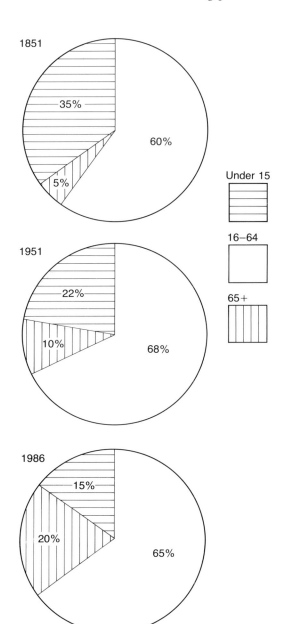

Age distribution of the population

3 a Explain the term 'age distribution'. *(1)*
  b What main trends can be identified from the data? *(2)*
4 a Suggest reasons for the increase in this century of the number of people in the population over the age of 65. *(2)*
  b Describe the main economic and social effects of an increasing proportion of older people in the population? *(6)*
5 'People in western industrial nations, like the UK, live longer than people in developing nations such as Africa'. Give reasons for this statement. *(3)*

Task 6 is based on the table below.

Year	Working population (millions)	Unemployed (000's)	Employed labour force (millions)
1975	25.9	840	25,060
1980	26.8	1,510	?
1987	27.9	2,995	?

6 a Explain the terms 'working population', 'unemployed' and 'employed labour force'. (3)
  b Calculate the size of the employed labour force in 1980 and 1987. (2)
  c Identify the main trends in the table and comment on your findings. (6)

Tasks 7–10 are based on the table below.

Occupational distribution of the population			
Percentage of employment in:	1950	1970	1987
Primary industries	10	5	3
Secondary industries	51	?	27
Tertiary industries	35	46	?
Unemployment	4	6	11

7 a Explain the term 'occupational distribution'. (1)
  b Give two examples of primary industries. (1)
  c Give two examples of secondary industries. (1)
  d Give two examples of tertiary industries. (1)
8 What percentage of the work force were employed in:
  a primary industries in 1950? (1)
  b secondary industries in 1970? (1)
  c tertiary industries in 1987? (1)
9 Using the figure for the working population in Task 6, calculate how many people were employed in primary industries in 1987. (2)
10 a Using the figures from the table, identify the changes which have taken place in employment since 1950. (3)
   b Explain the main reasons for these changes. (6)

Further development

The following ideas could be used to develop this assignment.

1 Organise a study of the population in your area.
2 Discuss why it is important for a business to be aware of changes in population trends.
3 Discuss the factors which affect the total size and structure of the population and then prepare a short essay giving, with reasons, your predictions of population trends over the next 25 years.

Assignment 3

International trade

Introduction

Assignment 3 is a set of exercises based on the UK's trade with other countries. It includes statistical data on the Balance of Payments and considers measures which the government can use to influence trade.

On completion of this assignment you should be able to:

1 understand the meaning and importance of overseas trade;
2 identify key features and recent trends from simple data;
3 identify the UK's main imports and exports;
4 understand the components and importance of the Balance of Payments;
5 appreciate the effects of government influences on international trade.

Background information

Few countries could ever be completely self-sufficient. This is because of the variety of different climates and geographical conditions, the availability of raw materials and labour, and of the capital investment necessary to provide a wide range of different goods and services. Therefore, most countries now specialise in producing what they can most cheaply and then trade. Specialisation and trade results in a higher standard of living, economies of scale and international co-operation.

UK trade with France

Goods and services bought from abroad are called **imports** and those sold abroad **exports**. The UK's main imports are food, raw materials and manufactured goods. The main exports are manufactured goods including machinery, vehicles and chemicals.

A nation must keep an account of its financial dealings with the rest of the world. This is called the **Balance of Payments**. It is a record of all the money which flows into or out of a country and it is rather like a bank account. If the account does not balance then the government may need to borrow money, repay loans or use its reserves to solve the problem.

The Balance of Payments is made up from three accounts.

1 The **Balance of Trade** or **visible balance**
   This is the difference in the value of all the actual goods which are imported and exported.
2 The **Balance on Current Account**
   This includes the visible balance and also the invisible items of trade, that is services such as transport, banking, tourism and insurance which are not physically taken in and out of the country.
3 The **Transactions in External Assets and Liabilities**
   This lists all the lending to, borrowing from, and investment between countries, trade credit and any other capital flows.

Adding together the totals on the Current Account and External Assets and Liabilities Account, gives the figure for the **Balancing Item**.

1986 Balance of Payments		
Current Account	£m	
Visibles	−8 254	
Invisibles	+7 154	
Current Balance		−1 100
UK External Assets and Liabilities		
Transactions in Assets	−86 964	
Transactions in Liabilities	+81 206	
Net Transactions		−5 758
Balancing Item	+6 858	

How the Balancing Item is calculated

Traditionally, Britain has suffered a visible trade deficit which has then been rectified to a large extent by an invisible trade surplus. Despite the benefits which trade brings, a country may still decide to restrict it in order to prevent problems like unemployment and 'dumping', to remain self-sufficient, to protect 'infant' industries or to solve its Balance of Payments problems. It may do this by introducing measures of **protection** through the use of tariffs, quotas, embargoes, subsidies and exchange controls.

Assignment

You are asked to work through the following tasks which are all related to international trade.

Tasks

1 Explain the meaning of 'international trade'. (1)
2 Using examples, give two reasons why countries trade with each other. (2)

For Task 3 you will need information from the latest edition of the *Annual Abstract of Statistics*.

3 The following table shows the main categories of UK imports and exports in 1985. Complete it with figures from a different year so that a comparison can be made in Task 5. (2)

Balance of Trade (£m)	Exports Year 1985	Imports Year 1985	Exports Year 19..	Imports Year 19..
Food, beverages and tobacco	4 970	9 274		
Basic materials	2 049	4 857		
Fuels and animal fats	17 373	11 049		
Chemical and related products	9 411	6 903		
Manufactured goods	10 422	14 348		
Machinery and transport equipment	24 684	26 899		
Miscellaneous manufactured goods	7 996	10 138		
Unclassified	1 991	1 322		
Total	78 051	80 162		
Balance of Trade				

(Source: adapted from 'External Trade', *Annual Abstract of Statistics: 1987*)

4 From the table identify:
   a the two main categories of UK imports in 1985; (1)
   b the two main categories of UK exports in 1985. (1)
5 Calculate the Balance of Trade for each of the two years chosen for comparison and state whether it was in surplus or deficit.
   a 1985 = (2)
   b 19.. = (2)
   c Which year was the most favourable for the UK? (1)

6 Complete the following table, which shows the UK's invisible trade items for 1985, with figures for a different year for comparison. (2)

Current Account (£m)				
Exports	1985	19..	Imports	1985 19..
Invisible receipts:			Invisible payments:	
Government Services	490			1 775
Sea Transport	3 272			4 429
Civil Aviation	3 188			2 835
Travel	5 451			4 877
Financial and other services	11 852			4 525
Interest, Profits and Dividends	53 032			49 632
Transfers	3 323			6 822
Total invisibles	80 608		Total	74 895
Balance of Invisible Trade				
Balance of Trade				
Balance on Current Account				

(Source: adapted from 'Balance of Payments', *Annual Abstract of Statistics: 1987*)

7 Calculate:
   a the Balance of Invisible Trade, and (1)
   b the Balance on Current Account for the two years compared. (1)
   c Why is a deficit on the Current Account more serious than a deficit on the Balance of Trade? (3)
8 The 1985 Balance of Transactions in External Assets and Liabilities showed a deficit of £7,296 million. Calculate the Balancing Item and indicate whether it is positive or negative. (2)
9 Complete the following sentences using the words:

   import export visible invisible increase decrease.

   a If more people go to Greece on holiday, then this will increase Greece's . . . . exports. (1)
   b If more people in the UK take foreign holidays, then this will increase the UK's . . . . (2)
   c If a Manchester company buys machinery from Switzerland, this will . . . . the UK's . . . . imports. (2)
   d American shareholders receiving dividends from ICI will . . . . the UK's invisible . . . . (2)
   e If British shipyards build a new liner for Australia this will . . . . the UK's . . . . (3)

15

10 Match the types of trade restriction in List A with the appropriate definitions in List B. (5)

List A Types of trade restriction
a Tariff
b Import quotas
c Subsidies
d Exchange control
e Embargo

List B Definitions
(1) A limit on the quantity of goods allowed into a country
(2) A ban on the import or export of goods usually for political reasons
(3) A limit on the amount of currency allowed to enter or leave a country
(4) A tax charged on imported goods
(5) Government payments to firms to prevent price rises

11 Consider the following government measures and suggest the likely effects on the Balance of Payments:
a participation in a World Trade Fair
b removal of all trade barriers
c increased tariffs on imports
d currency limit of £100 placed on tourists travelling abroad
e setting up a free insurance scheme for exporters (10)
12 What action can the government take if the Balance of Payments Account does not balance? (4)

Further development

The following ideas could be used to develop this assignment.

1 Using labels and advertisements, prepare a wall chart to indicate the importance of world trade to the UK.
2 Plot a graph showing the Balance of Payments position since the end of the Second World War.
3 Collect newspaper articles to illustrate trends/developments in the Balance of Payments and include the importance of North Sea Oil and changes in the exchange rates.
4 On a world map show which countries export, and which countries import some of the basic raw materials like tin, cotton, wool, tea, coffee.

Assignment 4

Introduction

Assignment 4 is a library and homework project on the European Community. It can be undertaken as an individual or group activity.

On completion of this assignment you should be able to:

1 identify the member countries of the European Community (EC);
2 describe the effect on UK consumers and businesses of EC membership;
3 explain the aims of EC policy.

Background information

The European Community (EC) or Common Market is a customs union which was originally established in 1957 by France, West Germany, Italy, Belgium, Luxemburg and the Netherlands. On 1 January 1973, the UK, Eire and Denmark joined to be followed by Greece in 1981, and Portugal and Spain in 1986. The Community now has a total population of over 350 million people.

The Community is basically a free trade area which in 1992 will become a political and economic whole governed by one central Parliament.

Meeting of the European Parliament in Strasbourg

European Community

Assignment

You are asked to work through the following tasks which are designed to develop your knowledge of the EC and its influence on the UK economy.

Member states of the European Community (EC), 1988

Tasks

1 On the map mark the member countries of the EC and show the size of each country's population. *(12)*
2 List the major industries of each country. *(12)*

B

3 In your own home complete the following table with 20 examples of goods produced in foreign countries. (5)
Note If you do not have a particular item, then choose a suitable alternative.

Commodity	Description	Country of origin
Packaged foods 1 2		
Tinned foods 3 4		
Fresh foods 5 6		
Clothing 7 8		
Shoes 9 10		
Car 11		
Furniture 12		
Domestic appliances, for example, 13 iron 14 razor 15 washing machine 16 fridge		
Other goods 17 18 19 20		

4 Comment on the results of your survey, drawing attention to the number and types of goods produced within the EC. (4)
5 Find out what percentage of UK trade takes place with EC countries. (1)
6 The EC is a customs union. Describe the two main features of such a union. (2)
7 Briefly explain how the EC budget operates. (2)
8 Give two advantages and two disadvantages for UK consumers of EC membership. (4)
9 Give two advantages and one disadvantage for UK businesses of EC membership. (3)
10 Describe five of the main aims of EC policy. (5)

Further development

The following ideas could be used to develop this assignment.

1 Study the Common Agricultural Policy and how it affects the price of food in the shops.
2 Examine the way in which the EC is organised and run.
3 Invite your local Euro-MP to talk about his/her work.
4 Collect newspaper and magazine articles about the EC and display them.

Assignment 5

Something to bank on

Introduction

Assignment 5 is in two parts. It begins with a local study of the services which banks, building societies and the Post Office provide for businesses and individuals. This is followed by a number of practical classroom exercises to show how a bank account operates. Part A is best carried out by working in small groups.

On completion of this assignment you should be able to:

1 identify the services offered by the banking system to both businesses and individuals;
2 appreciate the importance and growth of other financial institutions, for example building societies;
3 describe the money transfer services of the Post Office and the commercial banks;
4 explain how to open and operate a bank account.

Background information

The main **functions of banks** today are:

- to accept deposits and keep them safe for customers;
- to lend money to customers;
- to make and receive payments throughout the world.

They also provide a wide range of other services including loans, overdrafts, safe deposits, night safes, bankers drafts, bills of exchange, factoring and general financial advice.

Bank accounts

Banks offer their customers, businesses or individuals, a choice of two main types of account: deposit and current accounts. A third type is a **budget account** (see glossary).

A **deposit account** is used for savings by either individuals or firms who have spare cash. There are no bank charges and interest is paid on the balance in the account. Money can usually be withdrawn on demand although banks may ask for seven days notice for larger amounts.

Customers keep funds in a **current account** when they are needed for day-to-day use. They are given a cheque book which is used to make payments to others and to withdraw cash. Interest is not usually paid on the money, and bank charges may be incurred for the work done by the bank. Cheque cards are issued to reliable customers which guarantee that their cheques up to £50 will not 'bounce'. Withdrawals may also be made by standing order, direct debit, bank giro and a cash card. The bank sends customers regular statements showing the balance in their account.

Examples of bank services

Cheques

A cheque is simply a written instruction to a bank by a person with a current account to transfer money from their account to someone else's. The name of the person or company to whom the money is to be paid is called the **payee**. The **drawee** is the name of the bank, whilst the customer writing and signing the cheque is called the **drawer**.

An important feature of cheques is that they can be open or crossed. A crossed cheque is so called because it has two parallel lines across it. This means that it must be paid into a bank account. An open cheque can be cashed over the counter. Cheques can also be endorsed and passed to someone else. To endorse a cheque the payee signs his or her name on the back. This is helpful to someone who does not have a bank account but wishes to pay a cheque into a friend's account or into a building society.

Cash dispensing machines are now common and provide other facilities such as balance statements. The night safe is a more traditional service — who is likely to use it?

Assignment

You are asked to carry out some research and exercises based on the range of banking services currently available in the UK.

Tasks

Part A

Working in groups of two or three, visit a local shopping area and complete the following tasks. You will need to make rough notes which can be copied up later.

1 a List the commercial banks in the area. (2)
  b Obtain leaflets from at least one of them on the services offered. (1)
  c Make a list of five services which you and/or your family might use. Briefly explain each one. (5)

  d Name the two most common types of bank account and explain the differences between them. (2)
  e Find out what you would need to do to open a bank account. (2)
  f Find out which banking group is represented by each of the symbols below. (1)

2 a Obtain a leaflet from the nearest Post Office on the Girobank and briefly describe how it works. (2)
  b Give two instances when you and/or your parents might use the Giro system. (1)
  c Find out the value of all current Postal Orders and the poundage (Post Office charge) in each case. (3)
  d List and briefly describe three other services which are provided by the Post Office. (3)
3 Visit a building society and describe how its accounts and services differ from those which a bank offers. (3)

Part B

Tasks 4–8 are practical exercises to show how a bank account operates.

4 Assume that you wish to pay money into your current account. Using today's date complete the following paying-in slip and calculate the total amount paid in.

1 cheque for £10.00 3 x 50p pieces a £5 note
12 x £1 coins 2 x 20p coins 4 x 10p pieces
3 x 2p pieces 8 x 1p pieces

Your account number is 123678. Remember to complete the counterfoil. (4)

SPECIMEN ONLY Issued by Banking Information Service			
DATE_____	DATE_____	£50 notes . .	
CREDIT THE		£20 notes . .	
ACCOUNT OF_____	**MIDWEST BANK**	£10 notes . .	
£50 notes . .	**CREDIT**	£5 notes . .	
£20 notes . .		£1	
£10 notes . .		50p	
£5 notes . .		Silver . . .	
£1		Bronze . . .	
50p		**TOTAL CASH**	
Silver . . .		Postal Orders .	
Bronze . . .		Cheques, etc. . .	
TOTAL CASH		(listed overleaf)	
Postal Orders .	ACCOUNT	ACCOUNT NUMBER	£
Cheques, etc. .			
TOTAL CREDIT £	Paid in by_____	Customers are advised that the Bank reserves the right at its discretion to postpone payment of cheques drawn against uncleared effects which may have been credited to the account.	

5 Study the cheque below and answer the questions related to it:

```
1st. Nov.    1980.        🪷 MIDWEST BANK                              19
                             High Street,
                             SANDWALL                          40-21-01

J. Mc CALL
                         Pay    J. McCALL                              or Order

                         Twenty-four pounds    50p          £

£ 24-50

      100338        ⑈100338⑈ 20⑈386E⑈  13608873⑈
```

(On cheque, vertical text: A/C PAYEE ONLY)

a Midwest Bank is the:
- payer
- payee
- drawer
- drawee

b J. McCall is the:
- payer
- payee
- drawer
- drawee

c The cheque is incomplete. What items of information are required before J. McCall's bank will accept it?

d Why would J. McCall be unable to endorse the cheque and pass it to his friend P. Drake?

e Why does the number 100338 appear on both the cheque and the counterfoil? (5)

6 Complete the tasks related to the following bank statement.

a Calculate the balance for the 18 December and 21 December. (2)

b Briefly explain the difference between a standing order and a direct debit as shown on the statement. (1)

c Explain the meaning of the item 10.57 DR on 20 November. (1)

d Name two items which would be included in the term 'sundries'. (1)

e Briefly describe how a cash card is used. (2)

P Hamer 11 Sandwell Road Birmingham		In account with Midwest Bank High Street Sandwell Account No 0193257		
Date	Details	Payments	Receipts	Balance
198.				
20 Nov	Balance brought forward			10.57DR
21 Nov	Sundries		100.00	89.43
25 Nov	711034	20.00		69.43
28 Nov	711033	10.00		59.43
30 Nov	Borough of Sandwell	610.00		669.43
1 Dec	Cash Card	30.00		639.43
2 Dec	Scot. Amic. Ins. Co DD	31.00		608.43
3 Dec	Birmingham Phone SO	45.00		563.43
4 Dec	711035	300.00		263.43
10 Dec	Sandwell Squash Club SO	22.50		240.93
17 Dec	711036	90.00		150.93
18 Dec	Charges	9.60		?
21 Dec	Sundries	45.00		?

7 a Using a simple diagram, describe the operation of the cheque clearing system. (2)
  b Explain the difference between a bank loan and an overdraft. (1)
  c Describe what you understand by 'interest' on borrowed money. (1)
  d Describe how a business may make use of a bank account and other banking services. (2)
  e Outline three possible sources of finance that might be available to a business which wishes to enlarge its premises and buy additional equipment. (3)

Further development

The following ideas could be used to develop this assignment.

1 Invite the manager from a local building society or bank to talk about financial services.
2 Practise completing cheques and other banking forms such as standing orders and direct debits.
3 Collect three items of interest concerning finance which appear in local or national newspapers. Consider how each of these might affect the area where you live.
4 Study the functions of the Bank of England and its role in controlling the banking system.

Assignment 6

Introduction

Assignment 6 is about the growing use of credit cards and automatic methods of payment for goods and services. It emphasises the increasing impact of new computerised technology on both consumers and businesses.

On completion of this assignment you should be able to:

1 identify different methods of payment;
2 explain how the credit card system operates;
3 explain the advantages and disadvantages of credit cards for businesses and consumers;
4 describe the effects of new technology on methods of payment.

Background information

At present there are a number of different methods which can be used to pay for goods and services. These include cash, cheques, standing orders and direct debits. An increasingly popular method of payment is the use of **credit cards**. These are small plastic cards which cardholders can use at any shop, restaurant, garage or other business which is authorised to accept them.

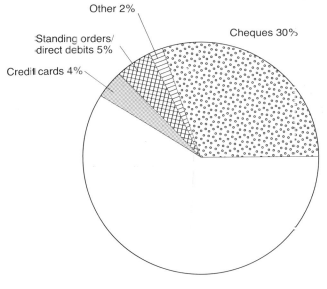

Other 2%
Standing orders/direct debits 5%
Credit cards 4%
Cheques 30%
Cash 59%

How payments are made

Cashless society

Using a credit card

When a credit card is presented in payment for goods or services the trader fills in the details on a sales voucher which the customer signs. The voucher is then placed in a small machine which imprints the details of the organisation and customer's card on the voucher. The customer receives one copy, the supplier keeps one and pays the third into the bank. The supplier's bank account is then credited with the payment. A small service charge (usually 5 per cent) is debited to the supplier's account.

Every month the cardholder is sent a statement which shows all the transactions for that month. If the account is settled in full, no interest is charged. Alternatively, only part of the balance may be repaid, in which case, interest is charged on the amount outstanding.

Future methods of payment

In the future it is likely that people and businesses will use cash and cheques to a lesser degree. More transactions will be settled by credit cards and new automatic methods of payment using computerised technology, examples of which are 'Connect' and 'Home and Office Banking'.

Examples of credit cards

Connect is a system of 'Electronic Funds Transfer at Point of Sale' (EFTPOS) introduced by Barclays Bank in June 1987. A Connect card can be used to pay for purchases in shops and other organisations which are members of the scheme. It is much quicker and simpler than using cheques because the cardholders account is debited immediately. Retailers pay a fixed charge for transactions accepted, but their bank account is credited immediately with the customer's payment.

Home and Office Banking as provided, for example, by both the Bank of Scotland and the Nottingham Building Society, uses a special device which links up with the bank's computer via a television set. Customers can key into the computer to transfer funds from one account to another, check their balance, pay bills, review standing orders and request a cheque book.

Realistically, we are unlikely ever to have a completely 'cashless society'. It would not be cost effective to use EFTPOS or a credit card to pay for a box of matches or a packet of envelopes. However, it is likely that banks will continue to encourage people to accept alternative methods of payment so that we will all use less and less cash. Yet at present 40 per cent of employees are still paid their wages in cash.

Assignment

Read the following extract from an article in the Observer *and then complete the tasks which are based on it.*

Britain's first credit card is 20 years old. JOANNA SLAUGHTER reports.

A credit card full house

BARCLAYCARD, the first credit card in this country was launched 20 years ago today.

'We were way ahead of the field in 1966,' says Peter Ellwood, Barclaycard's chief executive. 'It was quite a visionary thing to do.'

It was indeed, but unless the Barclaycard initiators were blessed with uncanny prescience, they could hardly have forecast what an oak tree was to grow out of their acorn.

In its first year Barclaycard signed up one million enthusiasts, and 30,000 retail outlets. Turnover was £10 million. By the end of last year there were 8.01 million card-holders, who had access to 235,000 retail outlets in the UK and 4.8 million worldwide. Annual turnover was £4.5 billion.

Business has been equally buoyant among Barclaycard's competitors. Access — the Joint Credit Card Company which has Lloyds, Midland, Nat West and Royal Bank of Scotland on board and which appeared six years after Barclaycard — now has 8.75 million card-holders. TSB Trustcard, an even later entrant, and like Barclaycard part of the VISA system, has 2.5 million aficionados.

In-store credit cards are also breeding with uncommon zeal, though their services are limited to designated shops and usually restricted to the purchase of goods. There are now more than 10 million store cards offered by some 1,500 retailers.

But perhaps the development which has done most to familiarise us with plastic cards is the wildfire spread of ATMs or cash-dispensers. There are around 7,000 in the country.

Banks still dominate the scene, but building societies have donned their running-shoes to make up lost ground. Halifax has its independent network of 360 Cardcash machines; Matrix, the first on-line network for leading building societies went live in February; and the Link group (including Abbey National and Nationwide, and the Co-op bank and National Girobank) expects to have 750 machines working by the end of the year.

Most ATM machines are now much more than simple cash-dispensers. You can deposit and

withdraw cash; check balances; order statements and, in some cases, pay your rates and electricity bills.

ATMs are a world-wide phenomenon, and reciprocal arrangements will mean that increasingly financial institutions will open up their machines to overseas visitors.

In January, for instance, there were 1,800 machines in Europe able to dispense cash to Barclaycard holders. Some 2,000 more will become operational in France and Spain this summer.

Another 'plastic card' development is a nationwide Electronic Funds Transfer at Point of Sale (EFTPOS) system. Pilot schemes are already running in some parts of the country.

With EFTPOS a plastic card (and the theory is that virtually all debit, credit and charge cards will be acceptable) will be used in electronic terminals in retailers and garages and the like, and the customers' bank or building society account will then be directly debited.

Another technological advance, to simplify credit card transactions, is Barclaycard's pilot scheme DARTS (Data Capture and Authorisation Retail Transaction Service). The electronic DARTS terminals authorise transactions automatically by telephone, collect all the data and store it on magnetic tapes.

'The evidence we've had so far is that the consumer likes the DARTS machine because it is quicker and gives more information on the receipt,' says Ellwood.

The proliferation of credit cards, though, is not without its critics. Some feel, not without reason, that the ready availability of the cards presents consumers with irresponsibly easy access to credit. After all, the Citizens Advice Bureaux was handling half a million debt inquirers a year ago.

'It does behove everyone in the credit industry to be extremely careful as to how and to whom they offer credit,' agrees Ellwood. Barclaycard turns down one in four applications, and Ellwood says 'this policy of selectivity is going to stay.'

Some claim, though, that there are retailers who are less fussy — some are now charging more than 30 percent for credit with staggeringly little consumer resistance from customers.

The only advice for consumers is to be strong-minded, and to try and ensure that the outstanding balance owing on a credit card is not allowed to drag on for months, as it then becomes expensive. Those who feel the cards are really providing too much temptation should tear their piece of plastic into small bits.

Another fear engendered by the proliferation of credit cards is the problem of fraud.

WHERE YOUR CARD BUYS MOST

Trade area	No. of outlets	Turnover £m
Petrol/garages/car hire	22,434	1,040
Department stores	2,141	380
Tour operators/travel agents	6,314	298
Hotels/motels	9,328	275
Ladieswear	19,229	242
Restaurants/nightclubs	17,796	234
Radio/TV	11,528	226
Menswear	12,308	198
Furnishers	8,213	173
Footwear	8,445	129

Source: Barclaycard

Tasks

1 a Explain the meaning of 'credit'. (2)
  b What is the name of the UK's first credit card and when was it introduced? (2)
  c Name the other major UK credit card company. (1)
  d In what types of businesses are credit cards used most? (2)
2 a Explain the main uses of Automated Teller Machines (ATMs). (2)
  b Using examples, explain why a customer would be interested in an 'on-line' network for ATMs. (4)
3 Describe briefly how the credit card system works from the point of view of the business accepting them and the consumer using them. (5)
4 How does the credit card company make a profit from its business? (2)
5 What are:
  • the likely *advantages*, and,
  • the likely *disadvantages* of credit cards for both businesses and consumers. (8)
6 a What do the initials EFTPOS and DARTS represent? (2)
  b What effect will these developments have on methods of payment in the future? (3)
7 a How many retailers now have their own credit cards? (1)
  b Name two retailer credit cards. (2)
  c Give reasons why you think they have been introduced. (4)
8 'As far as customers are concerned, one credit card looks much like another and performs the same function.'
  a Comment on this statement. (5)
  b Consider the ways in which companies offering credit cards can compete with each other. (5)

Further development

The following ideas could be used to develop this assignment.

1 Compare the use of credit cards with other methods of consumer credit such as hire purchase, trading checks and deferred payments.
2 Consider the effects on employment patterns of the increased use of 'cashless' methods of payment.
3 Discuss the possible effects on society of the increasing use of new technology in businesses and the home, for example, 'armchair shopping'.

Multiple choice 1

This section contains a series of questions or incomplete sentences followed by four possible responses. In each case select the most appropriate answer.

1 Which of the following statements about the division of labour is *not* true?
 a It enables costs to be reduced.
 b It results in a reduction in output.
 c Quality is improved as 'practise makes perfect'.
 d Training is usually quicker.

2 Which of the following is *not* a factor of production?
 a Money
 b Land
 c Labour
 d Enterprise

3 Complete the following diagram:

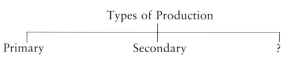

 a Tertiary
 b Commerce
 c Direct
 d Trade

4 The main purpose of production is to:
 a make more goods
 b provide employment
 c satisfy people's needs
 d build more factories.

5 The final link in the chain of distribution is the:
 a consumer
 b manufacturer
 c wholesaler
 d retailer.

6 If demand for a product increases, but supply remains the same, its price:
 a will rise
 b will fall
 c be unaffected
 d cannot be determined from this information.

7 The supply of labour will be increased by all the following factors except:
 a a higher birth rate
 b a lower death rate
 c increased immigration
 d increased emigration.

8 A country has its optimum population when:
 a it is overpopulated
 b it is underpopulated
 c it is making the maximum use of its resources
 d its population is always increasing.

9 The economic effects of an ageing population include all the following points except:
 a a less mobile work force
 b an increased dependency on the working population
 c a decrease in the average age of the population
 d changes in the patterns of demand.

10 Which of the following is an invisible trade item?
 a Tourism
 b Motor vehicles
 c Chemicals
 d Textile equipment

11 The UK government may use all except which *one* of the following to promote exports?
 a Organising trade fairs
 b Assessing potential markets
 c Introducing measures of protection
 d Help with foreign documentation.

12 Which of the following countries is *not* a member of the European Community?
 a France
 b Spain
 c Greece
 d Denmark

13 The reasons for a country deciding to impose barriers to trade may include all of the following except:
 a to prevent dumping
 b to reduce unemployment
 c to correct a balance of payments problem
 d to increase the level of imports.

14 A building society does *not*
 a provide loans for house purchase
 b offer savings accounts for investors
 c compete with banks for business
 d operate in the secondary sector of the economy.

15 If a cheque is not presented for payment within six months of the date on which it was drawn, it is said to be:
 a dishonoured
 b post-dated
 c stale
 d endorsed.

16 A bank loan is:
 a free of interest
 b a fixed amount for a fixed period
 c a fluctuating amount for a fixed period
 d only available to deposit account holders.

17 Which of the following is *not* a form of credit?
 a Standing order
 b Credit card
 c Overdraft
 d Mortgage

In each of the following questions, one or more of the responses is/are correct. Choose the appropriate letter which indicates the correct version.

a If 1 only is correct.
b If 3 only is correct.
c If 1 and 2 only are correct.
d If 1, 2 and 3 are correct.

18 The geographical mobility of labour depends on:
1 family ties
2 the age structure of the population
3 the availability of work in different areas.

19 Which of the following statements is/are true?
1 A standing order is the same as a direct debit.
2 A cheque card is given to everyone who opens a current account.
3 Girobank is a banking system operated through the Post Office.

20 Which of the following terms is/are associated with cheques?
1 Poundage
2 Third party
3 Current account

Business structure and organisation

Assignment 7

Introduction

Assignment 7 is a library research project. Working individually or in groups you are asked to carry out an investigation into the different types of business organisations which exist in the UK today.

On completion of this assignment you should be able to:

1 distinguish between controlled, free and mixed economies;
2 state the main types of organisation in the private and public sectors;
3 describe the main features of each type of organisation;
4 outline the main arguments for and against public sector activities.

Background information

We would all like to have more or better possessions than we have now, for example, better clothes, holidays, cars or houses. There is always something which we want but cannot have because our resources are scarce or limited. We only have a limited amount of money and therefore must choose carefully how best to spend it.

All societies in the world have limited resources and therefore face this basic economic problem of scarcity and choice. How the decision on the use of resources is made will depend on the type of economic system which operates in the country.

Economic systems can be centrally controlled, free or mixed. In a cen-rally **controlled** or communist economy, the state owns the resources and decides what should be produced. In a **free** or market economy, resources are owned by individuals who organise them to produce what people want to buy. However, most countries in the world actually have a **mixed** economy. This means that some resources and business organisations are owned privately and controlled by individuals or groups of individuals, and some publicly by the government as the following diagrams show. The **private sector** of the economy comprises many different types and sizes of businesses which are all run essentially for profit. These are:

PRIVATE SECTOR

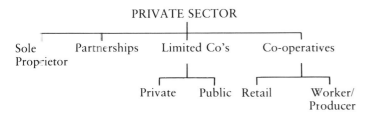

Who owns the business?

- **Sole Proprietors** individuals running their own business;
- **Partnerships** consisting of 2–20 people;
- **Private Limited Companies** which have limited liability and a minimum of two shareholders;
- **Public Limited Companies** which have a minimum of £50,000 capital raised by selling shares to the public which can then be bought and sold on the Stock Exchange;
- **Co-operatives** which can be either retail or producer;
- **Franchise** where a company helps to establish people in business using its name and products or processes. This is a more recent and rapidly growing form of business ownership.

PUBLIC SECTOR

```
                    PUBLIC SECTOR
        ┌────────────────┼────────────────────┐
    Public          Government          Municipal undertakings
  corporations      departments           (local authorities)
```

Public sector businesses are those which are owned and controlled by the government on behalf of the nation. They can be considered under three broad categories:

- **Public corporations** which can be set up directly by the government, as with the British Broadcasting Corporation (BBC) and British National Oil Corporation (BNOC) or as the result of nationalisation, for example, British Coal and British Rail.
- **Government departments** such as the Royal Mint and HMSO, which provide a variety of services.
- **Municipal undertakings** or **local authorities** who provide a range of services such as schools, libraries and parks. They also engage in trading activities, for example, leisure and entertainment centres.

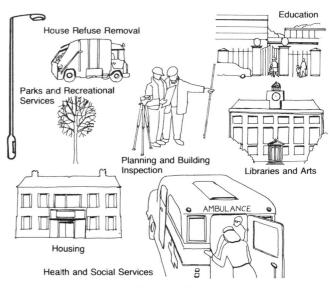

Some of the services provided by a local authority

Assignment

The background information outlines the basic differences between the private and public sectors of the economy. You are now asked to carry out a detailed study by completing the following tasks.

1 Explain, with examples, the difference between 'centrally controlled' , 'free' and 'mixed' economies. (6)
2 Copy and complete the table below. (8)
3 State which type of business organisation is most likely to be set up in the following situations:
  a A factory due to close is being kept open by the workers.
  b Mary Bryman wishes to open a health food shop, but feels she needs the support of a larger organisation.
  c Three doctors decide to work together.
  d A successful limited company needs extra capital for expansion.
  e A plumber decides to work for himself. (5)
4 a Give two advantages and two disadvantages of running your own business. (4)
  b Why are the businesses of sole traders usually quite small? (2)
  c What do you think would be the main advantages of a sole trader entering into a partnership? (2)
5 'Without limited liability it would be impossible for companies to raise large sums of capital.' Explain and comment on this statement. (4)
6 a Outline the main arguments for and against public enterprise. (4)
  b Explain, with examples, the meaning of privatisation. (3)

7 Identify the public corporations in the following box:

> British Gas   British Rail   British Airways
> British Petroleum   Trustee Savings Bank
> Marks and Spencer   Associated British Ports
> British Steel   Training Commission
> National Exhibition Centre

(1)

8 a Name three possible sources of finance for a local authority. (3)
  b List the main services and main trading activities provided by your local council. (4)
  c Describe any services or activities which you feel could be provided by private sector businesses and give reasons for those which you choose. (4)

Further development

The following ideas could be used to develop this assignment.

1 Prepare arguments for and against the privatisation of a public corporation such as the BBC or British Rail.
2 Discuss the main features of franchising and say why it is a growing form of business organisation.
3 Consider the main differences between retail and producer co-operatives.

Tasks

Type of business organisation	How many owners can it have?	What type of liability has it got?	Main sources of capital	Who owns it?	Who is responsible for its day-to-day running?	How are profits or losses shared?
Sole proprietor						
Ordinary partnership						
Private limited company						
Public limited company						
Retail co-operative						
Workers co-operative						
Franchise						
Public corporation						

Assignment 8   **A local business study**

Introduction

Assignment 8 is a detailed study of a local business organisation. It involves working in groups to collect information and produce an illustrated project.

On completion of this assignment you should be able to:

1 understand the main features and objectives of a business organisation;
2 appreciate the reasons for the location of local businesses;
3 recognise the importance of a business to the local community;
4 apply your knowledge of business concepts to a practical situation.

Background information

There are many different types and sizes of businesses which have developed to supply the wide variety of goods and services which people want to buy. Some of these businesses are in the private sector of the economy and others are in the public sector. Whatever the type of organisation, each has certain **objectives** which it seeks to achieve.

The main objective of **private sector** organisations is usually to achieve maximum **profits**. Other important objectives will vary from firm to firm. Thus, for example, a new business might see **survival** as its main objective in the first year of trading, followed by **consolidation**, and it may be some years before it becomes very profitable. On the other hand, a larger firm may seek to increase its **market share** (by taking more of the total sales of a product or service than its competitors), or seek to achieve future **growth** by developing a wider range of products.

Public sector organisations also seek to make profits, but their first concern is to **operate for the benefit of the nation**. This may involve operating some unprofitable services in the public's interest, for example, rail services in country areas or uneconomic coal mines in areas of high unemployment.

The successful running of any business, no matter how large or small, involves the co-ordination of many different functions. When an organisation is small, one person can often control it. That person is able to do all the important jobs such as purchasing, accounts and marketing, and is very closely involved in the day-to-day running of the firm. As a firm grows, however, one person may be too busy to do everything and therefore may need to bring in a partner or employ extra staff to carry out some of the work.

This process of growth and specialisation of jobs within the business may continue as a firm develops into a private or public limited company. When this happens, the shareholders will elect a board of directors to make policy decisions and to run the business on their behalf.

Business objectives

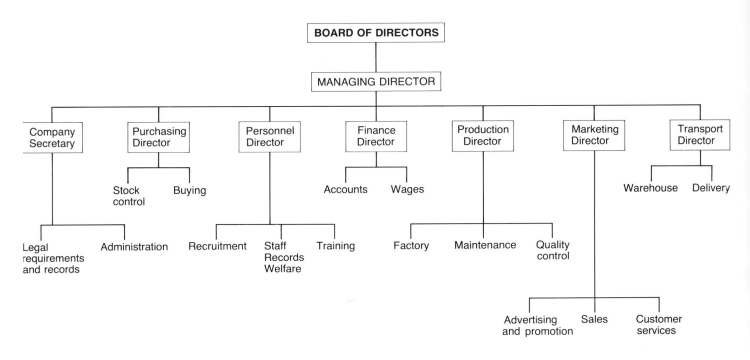

The 'organisation chart' shows how a typical business may be structured

As the organisation chart shows, the Board will usually appoint a managing director as head of the business. Specialist departments are usually established with a director in overall charge of each function. The actual number of departments will depend on the size of the firm and could include purchasing, finance, production, marketing, personnel and transport.

This pyramid structure is known as **line management**, that is, instructions in the organisation are passed along lines in the hierarchy (usually downwards). Within an organisation there may also be specialist advisory or support services such as legal advice or computer services. Frequently these service several departments and therefore are referred to as **staff functions**.

Assignment

Working in groups you are asked to discover as much information as possible about different types of local business organisations. Each group should study a different business, produce an illustrated project and make a presentation for the benefit of the other groups.

Collecting information about local businesses

Tasks

1 Contact the Head Office of the business you have chosen to study and ask for further information about it. Useful sources of information might include the employees' handbook, advertising or promotional literature and, for public limited companies, a copy of their annual accounts. Try to arrange a personal visit and keep a copy of your letter to include in your project.

2 From the information you receive, plus articles in the press, local history books or other relevant material, write about the business concerned. Interviews with past or present employees will also help you.

3 The following are guidelines intended to help you to plan your project and to give an indication of the information which you should include.

a **Location**
  - Draw a map to show the location of your town in the United Kingdom.
  - Prepare a simple plan of the town and mark on it the situation of the firm chosen.
  - Describe this situation. What advantages and disadvantages does it have?
  - What government grants (if any) have influenced the location?

b **History**
  - Write a brief history of the company (and/or the group of companies to which it belongs), including the reasons for its location.

c **Raw materials**
  - Describe the type of raw materials which the firm uses and where they come from.

d **Products**
  - Describe the type of products made and (if possible) their prices. Include photographs, illustrations or drawings.

e **Finance**
  - Give details of the amount and type of capital, if this can be found out, from the information obtained.

f **Marketing**
  - *Markets* Show the location of the firm's markets, at home, and abroad (if appropriate). A diagram or illustration would be helpful. Now describe the methods of:
  - *Market research* How are the markets identified?
  - *Advertising and sales promotion* Consider the amount and types of advertising and sales promotion used, include examples.
  - *Pricing* How are prices set?
  - *Packaging* What types of packaging are used and why?
  - *Distribution* How do the products get to the market?
  - *Transport* What types of transport are used and why?

g **Turnover**
  - Give details of the firm's sales and compare the figures for at least two years. Comment on the trend.

h **New technology**
  - Describe the impact of computing, word processing, robotics or other developments on the business.

i **Organisation structure**
  - With the use of a diagram, describe how the firm is organised.

j **Staff**
  - Consider the number and type(s) of staff employed: how are they recruited, what are their hours of work, their training, holidays and working conditions?
  - Describe the provision of any staff facilities, for example, a canteen or the organisation of sports and social activities.
  - Include any information you can find about the trade unions to which staff might belong.

k **Future developments**
  - Discuss the present and future objectives and projects for the company, such as proposed new products.

l **Other**
  Record any other interesting information, for example:

  - Is the business expanding or contracting? Give reasons for your answer.
  - Does it take on YTS trainees or young people for work experience?
  - How is it influenced by local and central government?

4 Present a report in an interesting and attractive way, including a list of all references used. A suitable structure might be as follows:
  a Title and purpose of report
  b Summary
  c Introduction
  d Body of report, that is, presentation and analysis of data collected
  e Conclusions or results. (50)

Further development

The following ideas could be used to develop this assignment.

1 The project could continue throughout the course. Each group could get itself 'adopted' by a business and go back to it periodically to obtain practical knowledge and experience.
2 An alternative project could be for each group to select a manufacturing and a service industry, compare the two and draw conclusions.
3 Where practical, the project could be extended to include stock control.
4 Explain the difference between 'line' and 'staff' organisation in the firm; include a discussion of the importance of authority, responsibility and delegation.

c

Assignment 9

Shopping around

Introduction

Assignment 9 is in two parts. It begins with a practical survey of different types of retail outlets. This is followed by a number of classroom exercises based on the role of wholesalers. Part A is best carried out working in small groups although you should each produce your own written work.

On completion of this assignment you should be able to:

1 understand the chain of distribution;
2 describe the main types of wholesalers and their functions;
3 explain the main features of different retail outlets;
4 describe the main methods of retailing without shops.

Background information

The process of getting goods from manufacturers to consumers is called the **chain of distribution**. As the following diagram shows, it can involve both wholesalers and retailers.

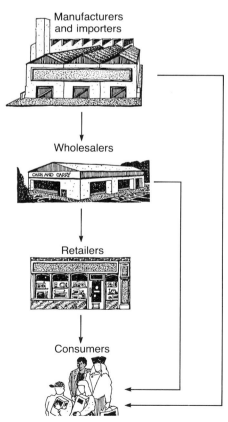

Manufacturers and importers

Wholesalers

Retailers

Consumers

The chain of distribution

Wholesalers are often described as **middlemen** because they are the middle link in the chain of distribution. They buy goods in bulk (large quantities) from manufacturers and sell them in smaller quantities to retailers. The goods are stored in a warehouse until required.

The retail trade is referred to as the last link in the chain of distribution because it brings goods and services to the final consumer who will not resell them.

There are four main types of **wholesalers**:

- **Traditional wholesalers** collect orders from retailers, deliver the goods and allow trade credit.
- **Cash and carry wholesalers** are rather like supermarkets where retailers go to buy their goods and pay cash at the exit.
- **Voluntary** or **symbol groups** consist of a number of independent retailers who join together with a local wholesaler to enable him to buy in bulk from manufacturers. This leads to lower prices and it helps them to compete with bigger organisations. Sometimes a number of voluntary groups join together throughout the country to form voluntary chains, for example, Mace, Spar and VG.
- **Co-operative Wholesale Society (CWS)** is the largest wholesaler in the UK and supplies goods for co-operative retail societies.

Several factors have led to a decline in the number of wholesalers, in particular, the development of large retail organisations which are able to buy goods themselves directly from manufacturers.

Inside a Sainsbury's store, a supermarket mostly selling foodstuffs

There are many different types of **retailers** each of which provides particular services for consumers.

- **Independent traders** offer personal counter service but their prices are often higher than other shops.
- **Self-service stores** are often independent but frequently join group wholesalers like Spar or VG to enable them to compete with larger shops.
- **Supermarkets** offer cut prices and a wider choice of goods.
- **Superstores and hypermarkets** are very large stores, usually located away from town centres, which sell a vast range of merchandise.
- **Department stores** are found in the centre of large towns or cities and offer a large range of goods and have facilities such as toilets and restaurants.
- **Multiple retailers** (those with more than 10 branches) specialise in selling a wide variety of one particular type of merchandise.
- **Variety chain stores** are multiples which sell a variety of goods.
- **Discount stores** concentrate on selling durable household goods at cut prices.
- **Co-operative stores** are best known for the dividend which they give to customers.
- There are also many methods of retailing **without using shops** including markets, mail order, mobile 'shops', door-to-door selling, party selling, automatic vending machines and trade fairs and exhibitions.

Assignment

You are asked to carry out some library research and a practical survey which will enable you to study the role of wholesalers and compare the differences between the main types of retail outlets in the UK.

Tasks

Part A

Working in pairs or small groups visit a local shopping area and complete the following tasks. You will need to make rough notes which can be copied up later. Before your visit you will need to complete tasks 1–3.

1 Select two retail outlets out of each section below:
   a F W Woolworth   Marks and Spencer
     British Home Stores   Littlewoods
     W.H. Smith   Boots
   b Safeway   Sainsbury's   Liptons   ASDA
     Fine Fare   Tesco   Co-op   Kwik Save   Gateway
   c Debenham's   Lewis's   Selfridge's   Harrod's
     Kendal Milnes   Owen Owen   Rackhams
   d Chelsea Girl   Miss Selfridge's   Burtons
     Richard Shops   Fosters   Paige
     Dorothy Perkins   Next   C & A Modes
   e A local independent newsagent and a local 'corner shop'.

2 Use the following 12 questions for your survey and add *three* of your own.
   1 Is the store self-service?
   2 Are any items in the store served over the counter? If so, which?
   3 Are baskets and/or trolleys used in the store?
   4 How are the prices shown on goods?
   5 How are the items arranged in the store? Are they, for example, on rails or fixtures?
   6 What other selling techniques are evident? Are there, for example, special offers or free samples?
   7 Are credit cards such as Access and Visa accepted?
   8 Where do customers pay for goods? Are there, for example, checkouts at the exit?
   9 Does the store offer its own credit facilities to its customers?
   10 Are there carpets on the floor?
   11 Is music playing in the background?
   12 Does the store deliver goods?

3 Design a chart which you can use to record the answers to your questions. A suggested layout might be as follows:

Type of Store	Variety Chain Store		Multiple Grocery Supermarket		Department Store		Multiple Clothing		Independents	
	1	2	3	4	5	6	7	8	9	10
Name of Store										
1. Is the store self-service?										
2. Are any items in the store served over the counter? If so, which?										

4 Visit the shops you have selected and carry out your survey.
5 Prepare a brief report on the findings from your survey. Comment on the differences which you found between the various types of retail outlets. Suggest reasons for these differences. A suitable structure might be as follows:
   a Title and purpose of report
   b Summary of findings
   c Introduction
   d Body of report, that is, presentation and analysis of data collected
   e Conclusions or results.   (50)

Part B

Read the background information carefully and then complete tasks 6–12. You may need to use a library or other sources of information to help you.

6 What is meant by the 'chain of distribution'?   (2)
7 Why are wholesalers sometimes described as 'middlemen'?   (2)
8 How do wholesalers help manufacturers?   (4)
9 a Wholesalers *break bulk* for retailers and some allow *trade credit*. Explain what each of these terms means.   (4)
   b Why do many large retail organisations not require the services of wholesalers?   (2)
10 a Give four *local* examples of voluntary groups and/or chains.   (4)
    b What are the advantages to a customer of buying at a shop which belongs to a voluntary group or chain?   (4)
11 Why are wholesalers generally less important today than they used to be?   (4)
12 a Name and briefly describe five methods of retailing without shops.   (10)
    b Suggest two advantages and two disadvantages of each for customers.   (10)
    c Explain the terms 'loss leaders' and 'impulse buying' and say why they are important in retailing.   (4)

Further development

The following ideas could be used to develop this assignment.

1 Discuss the different types of markets such as retail, wholesale, produce, commodity, shipping, insurance, financial and foreign exchange.
2 Describe different methods of trading including auctions, ring trading, private deals, 'spot' and 'futures' markets.
3 Markets with many buyers and sellers operate according to the laws of supply and demand. Briefly explain these laws.

Assignment 10

Introduction

Assignment 10 is a practical research survey. It will help you to understand the key factors which influence the location of a small business. It is best carried out as a group exercise although you should each produce your own report.

On completion of this assignment you should be able to:

1 describe some of the measures used to analyse a potential business location;
2 appreciate how competition affects the choice of a business location;
3 explain how other types of businesses will influence the choice of site.

Background information

There are many reasons why firms or industries are located in a particular place. **Primary or extractive industries** have little choice in their location. Hence coal mining, quarrying, forestry and oil drilling must take place where the raw materials are found. Likewise, fishing must be near to fishing grounds and harbours, agriculture must be where the land and climate is suitable.

Secondary or **manufacturing industries** will usually seek a site which offers the lowest costs of production and distribution. Hence they may be located either near to the sources of raw materials which are used or near to the markets where the goods are sold. For example, steel manufacturing requires large quantities of bulky raw materials like iron ore, coal and limestone and therefore firms are located near to supplies of these materials. On the other hand, soft drinks manufacturers are usually found near to their markets because the cost of transport is often higher than the costs of production.

Tertiary or **service industries** are usually located near to the market where the demand exists. Hence shops, garages and banks are all found where there are a lot of people who will use them, for example, there would be no point in siting a large petrol station on an isolated country road because there would be insufficient passing trade. Hypermarkets, however, are frequently sited away from city centres but still within easy reach of large centres of population because customers are attracted by their low prices and wide range of goods.

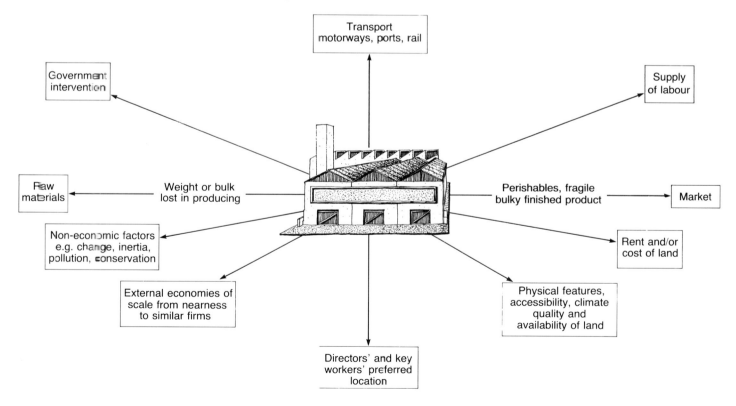

Factors influencing the location of a business

As the diagram shows, many other factors may also affect the location of a business including the availability of suitable labour and whether government assistance is available. For example, financial help may be provided towards the cost of buildings or equipment, ready built factories may be offered at very low rent, or tax incentives may be given to firms who locate in a particular area.

Many industries today are referred to as being **footloose**. This is because the development of new and improved sources of power, raw materials and transport means that they no longer have to locate near to raw materials or markets. Instead they can choose to go where they like.

Assignment

Read the situation below and complete the tasks that follow. This will show you one way of approaching the problem of where best to locate a shop in the area where you live.

If you were considering opening a shop you would need to try to determine the best position in your area for the type of business concerned. You would find that some locations are likely to be more successful than others. To look at this problem in more detail, assume that you wish to set up a small local business. You could, for example, decide to sell fruit and vegetables, provide office services, hire video films or print tee-shirts. You have a choice of three possible sites. These are shops which you should assume are likely to become empty in the near future.

1 Next door to a bank, for example, Barclays or Lloyds.
2 Next door to a multiple retailer, for example, Dixons or Boots.
3 Next door to a building society, for example, Halifax or Woolwich.

For your study, you may prefer instead to use shop sites which are currently vacant.

To start your business you will need to borrow some money from a bank. However, before going to see the bank manager you will need to collect a lot of information.

Which site would you choose?

Tasks

Working in groups or pairs you should visit a local shopping area and complete the following tasks.

1 Draw a rough sketch indicating the shops and other businesses in the area:
  a by name, for example, Smiths, Oyston;
  b by type of business, for example, jewellers, estate agents.
2 a Mark the three proposed sites clearly on the sketch.
  b Show the bus stops/station(s), car parks, railway station(s), pedestrian crossings, traffic free areas.
  c At a later date, copy up the sketch neatly.
3 Examine the area around each of the three proposed sites, making notes under the following headings:
  a **Situation**
  For example, in the main shopping precinct, market square, corner of the High Street.
  b **Condition of property**
  Old, new, needs repairing, good condition.
  c **Competition**
  i.e. nearby shops selling similar goods. Mention these by name and briefly describe the type of competition which they represent.
  d **Size of property**
  If possible measure, if not estimate, the size of:
  Exterior • total width of the shop front
           • the window space
  Interior • the area of the floor space
           • other space, for example, is there space suitable for storage at rear or upstairs?
  Plan   Draw a rough sketch of each site to show the above details. Later copy this up neatly to scale.
  e **Location of other important retailers/focal point(s)**
  For example, being near to Marks and Spencer's or Woolworth's means that a lot of people are likely to pass the site and it will be easier to find.
  f **Rents and rates**
  Make some enquiries with the local council or estate agents about the rent and rates paid by traders in the town. You will find that they are usually based on the size of the premises, its situation and how this is likely to affect the business. Explain which site you would expect to be most expensive.
  g **Advantages and disadvantages**
  List and briefly describe these for each site. For example,
  Advantage 1   As the site is next to a pedestrian crossing more people will pass it and notice the window display.
  h **Other information**
  For example, likely development(s) in the area and nearness of suppliers (wholesalers or manufacturers).

4 Carry out the following to discover the busiest location.
  a A pedestrian count to discover how many people pass each of the three sites during a particular period of time, say 1½ hours. Note the number of men, women and children and their approximate ages.
  b Note the number of customers entering adjoining premises.
  c Establish how many pedestrians pass on each side of the street. If one side is more popular, try to give reasons for this – is it sunnier, for example?
  d If appropriate conduct a traffic count – is the road likely to be difficult to cross?
  e From the information collected, prepare a grid of facts and figures. Further analysis using other methods might include graphs, pie charts, histograms and averages.
5 Your bank manager will want to know which of the three sites you feel is the best one and why. You have been told that usually this information is needed in writing.
  Present your complete findings in the form of an individual report to be given to your bank manager.
  A suitable structure might be as follows:
  a Title and purpose of report
  b Summary of findings
  c Introduction
  d Body of report, i.e. presentation and analysis of data collected
  e Conclusions or results   (50)

Further development

The following ideas could be used to develop this assignment.

1 It may be possible to invite a speaker from the Chamber of Commerce, the Small Firms Information Service, a local estate agent or the local council to talk about how they might help a new small business.
2 Once a site has been chosen, a business plan could be prepared.
3 This study could be adapted for a potential industrial location.

Scale of production

Introduction

Assignment 11 is a study of the factors which influence the size and growth of firms. It includes exercises on economies of scale, integration, diseconomies of scale and the survival of small firms.

On completion of this assignment you should be able to:

1 describe the reasons for, and the methods used to achieve, the growth of firms;
2 appreciate the significance of internal and external economies of scale;
3 identify the factors which limit the growth of firms;
4 explain why small firms survive.

Background information

As a firm expands, it can gain the advantages of operating on a larger scale. That is, the larger the output, the lower the cost per unit, because of what are called **economies of scale**. These advantages are of two types: **internal economies** which a firm gains directly by increasing the size of its own operations and **external economies** which arise indirectly, not from the growth of the firm, but from the growth of the size of the industry and its concentration in a particular area.

Internal savings can result from economies of scale in production and from financial, marketing, managerial and risk-bearing economies of scale. External economies can result from the availability of labour, the existence of ancilliary/support industries, marketing and distribution facilities, commercial services, and also from 'disintegration'.

However, it is also possible for a firm to grow too large. An increase in size can bring with it problems of management and control, communication and industrial relations. These problems can reduce a firm's efficiency and cause its average cost of production to increase. This is referred to as **diseconomies of scale**.

A firm can grow in size in one of two main ways. Either internally, by producing a wider range of products, or by opening more factories. Alternatively, it may take over or merge with another company.

When two or more firms combine together to form a larger unit, it is called **integration**. This can either be horizontal, vertical or lateral. **Horizontal integration** takes place when firms at the same stage of production combine together under the same management. **Vertical integration** is the amalgamation of firms in the same industry but at different stages of production. This may take place 'backwards' towards the source of its raw materials or 'forwards' towards its markets. **Lateral integration** occurs when firms with similar, but not competing products, merge together. This enables firms to diversify and offer a wide range of related products.

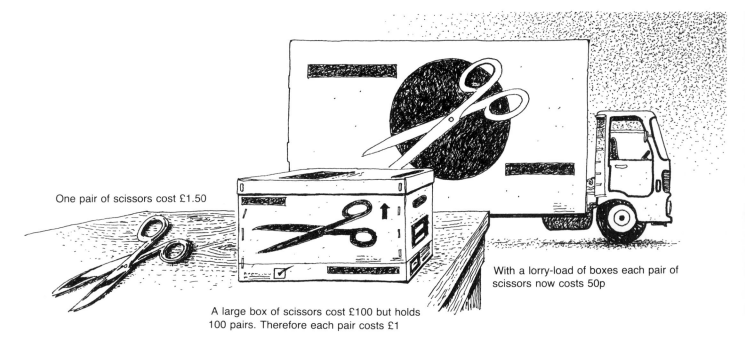

One pair of scissors cost £1.50

A large box of scissors cost £100 but holds 100 pairs. Therefore each pair costs £1

With a lorry-load of boxes each pair of scissors now costs 50p

An example of economies of scale (bulk buying)

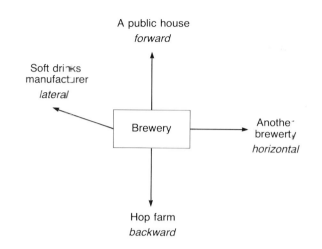

A public house
forward

Soft drinks
manufacturer
lateral

Brewery

Another
brewery
horizontal

Hop farm
backward

Integration

When one firm merges with or takes over another, it does so by buying all of the other's shares. However, sometimes a firm does not actually own another completely but still controls it by buying over 50% of its shares. Sometimes **holding companies** are formed just to take a controlling interest in other firms. Many large firms also expand by diversifying into a wide range of completely different product areas by buying a controlling interest in other firms. Often large **conglomerates** are formed where one firm controls many others. Some may expand further by buying foreign companies or opening divisions abroad so that many operate throughout the world. These are referred to as **multi-national companies**.

'*International*' *usually means the company is multinational*

Despite the advantages enjoyed by large firms, small firms still predominate in most forms of business. Small firms are especially important in certain industries such as agriculture, building, retailing and personal and professional services. It is also important to note that even within the same industry, firms often vary considerably in size.

Assignment

Read the background information and then complete the following tasks.

Tasks

1 From List A select the *three external economies of scale.* (3)
2 Match the remaining examples of economies in List A with the appropriate type of economy in List B.

List A Example of economies
a Computerisation of company records
b Machinery being fully utilised
c Buying raw materials at bulk prices
d Supply of suitable skilled labour in the area
e Spending more on advertising giving lower unit costs
f Introducing a Sales Department with its own manager
g Specialised courses at the local college
h Raising capital is easier and cheaper
i Ancillary firms supplying specialised machinery and components
j Manufacturing a wider range of products

List B Types of economies
1 Marketing
2 Managerial
3 Production
4 Financial
5 Risk-bearing

3 From the box below identify which *method of growth* each of the following examples represents:

> conglomerate   diversification   holding company
> horizontal   lateral   multi-national
> vertical-backwards   vertical-forwards

a A furniture manufacturer merges with an electronics company.
b Two retail jewellery chains merge together.
c A brewery takes over a metal can manufacturer.
d A chocolate company takes over a soft drinks manufacturer.
e A tea producer establishes an overseas division.
f A paper manufacturer gains effective control of a cosmetics firm.
g A brewery takes over the public houses which it supplies with beer.
h A weaving firm takes over a spinning company.
i A tobacco company takes over both a frozen food firm and a biscuit manufacturer.
j A British engineering firm buys two American competitors. (10)

4 List the names of at least two small local businesses under each of the following headings:
   a Professional services
   b Personal services
   c Retailing
   d Construction and related trades
   e Manufacturing   (5)
5 Complete the following sentences by inserting *large* or *small* as appropriate:
   a Photography businesses are usually . . . . because not much capital is required to start up.
   b Decorating firms tend to be . . . . because customers require personal attention.
   c Chemical companies are usually . . . . because of the high capital investment required.
   d Corner shops are . . . . because their owners frequently lack the capital for expansion.
   e Petrol companies are usually . . . . because of the benefits from economies of scale.   (5)
6 Identify two important features from the following table: (5)

Employees per firm	Number of firms	% of Total firms	Total number of employees (000s)	% of Total employed
1–19	25,000 (Est)	43	125 (Est)	3
20–99	23,368	40	1,005 (Est)	21
100–999	9,048	16	2,382	50
over 1,000	589	1	1,258	26
TOTAL	58,005	100	4,770	100

(Figures based on *Annual Abstract of Statistics: 1986*)

Size of Manufacturing Units in the UK: 1984

Note: Information for units employing 1–19 is not provided therefore the above figures are estimated.

7 Suggest *five* factors which may give a large firm a competitive advantage over a smaller firm.   (5)
8 Now, using a local example, identify *five* ways in which a small business can successfully compete with a larger one.   (10)

Further development

The following ideas could be used to develop this assignment.

1 Using a recent example of a merger, discuss the economies of scale which should have resulted. Collect press articles and other media comment to form the basis of a class discussion or project. Suggest any likely diseconomies which might result from the merger.
2 Consider the possible effects on your school/college (or one nearby) of extending its opening hours by two hours per day/evening, or opening at weekends. Itemise the types of economies which might be achieved and any possible diseconomies.
3 Discuss the likely impact on the size of firms resulting from the introduction of new computerised technology.

Assignment 12

Introduction

Assignment 12 takes the form of a case study which illustrates the importance of capital in a business. It can be used for individual or group work.

On completion of this assignment you should be able to:

1 recognise the main sources of capital available to businesses;
2 state the main features of private and public limited companies;
3 describe how shares are bought and sold;
4 explain why share prices fluctuate.

Background information

Most people who start up in business need **capital**, for example, a window cleaner needs to buy a bucket, ladder and wash leather. A retailer needs premises and a stock of goods to sell, whilst a manufacturer needs a factory, machinery and raw materials as well as money to pay for wages, heat, light, advertising and transport in order to make and sell his goods. If a business is successful, more capital may be needed to enable it to expand or modernise its plant and equipment.

In the **short-term** a business can obtain capital by means of a bank loan or overdraft, by 'ploughing back' its profits or using trade credit. It might also be possible to lease equipment, furniture or vehicles or buy them on hire purchase.

Long-term capital may be obtained in a number of ways. In a small firm most of the capital required is provided by the businessman himself, possibly with the help of his family and friends or a long-term bank loan. A sole proprietor might also obtain more capital by bringing in partners or by forming a limited liability company.

Capital for limited companies is provided by shareholders. These are investors who own part of the business and in return for providing the money they receive a share of the profit called a **dividend**.

There are two types of company: **private** (Ltd) and **public** (plc). Both must have at least two shareholders but there is no maximum number. The main difference between them is that public limited companies can sell their shares to the public.

A shareholder is unable to get his money back from the company because it has already been spent on buildings, equipment, wages and all the other needs of the business. Therefore, the Stock Exchange provides a market where second-hand shares can be bought and sold.

Business finance

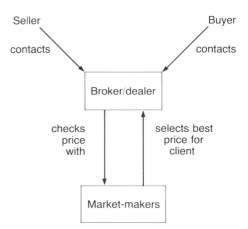

Note: A broker/dealer may also operate as a market-maker

Dealing in shares

Anyone wishing to buy or sell shares must instruct a broker/dealer to act on their behalf. The broker will try to get the best deal by checking the price(s) with the **market-makers** who operate rather like wholesalers. Market-makers display their prices on television screens via SEAQ (Stock Exchange Automated Quotations). This system is available throughout the country and shows a list of all market-makers with their prices for particular shares. These prices are adjusted daily in response to changes in supply and demand.

Two prices are shown, a higher one at which they will sell shares (**offer price**) and a lower one at which they will buy (**bid price**), for example, £1.55 and £1.45. When he has found the best price of the share being traded, the broker will then telephone the market-maker to complete the transaction.

Finance		
Abbey	237	+3
Barclays	460	+10
Hambros	232	
Hill Samuel	800	
Kleinwort	308	+5
Lloyds	253	+2
Midland	375	
Morgan Gren	255	−5
NatWest	548	
Pearl	345	+12
Royal Insur	380	−7
Sun Life	915	+4
TSB	110	
Union Dis	810	

Share prices as they appear in some newspapers

Note
1 The share price shown is usually a figure between the bid and offer price.
2 The second column shows the change in the share prices from the previous day.

The share prices of most public limited companies can be found in the *Financial Times*, whilst many other daily newspapers such as the *Daily Telegraph* and *Daily Mail* include shorter lists restricted to well known companies. Newspapers also write articles commenting on the trading results of companies.

Assignment

Having read the background information, study the press report below about the trading results of O'Connor International plc and complete the tasks that follow.

O'Connor Fights Back

What do the miners strike, riots in India and a fall in the value of the dollar have in common? They have all been responsible for knocking profits over the past few years at the engineering group O'Connor International plc.

The group was hard hit by the recession in the early 1980s and has been fighting to regain its markets ever since. O'Connor believes that the worst is now over and that once again it is poised for growth. However, this depends upon the health of the manufacturing industry and the general economic climate. The loss making Indian operation has been restructured, but the American market is still threatened by the dollar's weakness.

There is evidence of an improvement in the figures for the year to December with profits up 50% to £8.5 million, though they are still £2.5 million below the 1980 peak. A total dividend of 6.25p is being paid against 5p last year.

Power transmission, which accounts for half of sales, but a lot less in profits, has seen its 9,000 work force slashed by a third. It is also planning to double sales in Europe within three years.

Three quarters of the production from the conveyor belt division is sold to British Coal, so the year–long strike proved devastating. With mine closures still continuing, orders are unlikely to rise and exports offer the main opportunity for growth.

Group profits of £12m are expected this year. Overall the market seemed pleased and the shares ended 10p higher on the day at 120p.

Tasks

1 a Explain why a business needs capital. (2)
  b List three possible sources of capital, apart from his own funds, for a sole proprietor. (3)
2 Why is a shareholder said to 'own' part of a business? (2)
3 a Give the main features of public and private limited companies. (4)
  b Briefly explain one major difference between them. (2)

  c Is O'Connor International a public or private limited company? (1)
4 Briefly describe the procedure involved if you wanted to buy 600 shares in O'Connor International. (4)
5 Name the two trading divisions of the company. (2)
6 a What is the current price of O'Connor's shares? (1)
  b What was the previous day's price for the shares. (1)
7 a Explain what you understand by the term 'dividend'. (2)
  b Calculate the percentage increase in the dividend for the year. (2)
  c Calculate the dividend payable to Mary Williams who owns 2,000 shares in the company. (2)
8 a How much profit did the company make this year? (1)
  b What is the company's forecast profit for next year? (1)
  c What information is there in the article to suggest that the company will achieve this level of profit? (6)
9 The following chart shows the share price of O'Connor plc over a five year period.

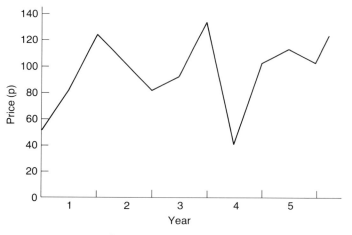

Share prices of O'Connor International plc

  a In which year was the company's share price at its highest and what was the price? (2)
  b In which year was the company's share price at its lowest and what was the price? (2)
10 Suggest some factors which are likely to affect the company's current and future share price. Explain your answer. (10)

Further development

The following ideas could be used to develop this assignment.

1 Visit the Stock Exchange Information Centre in London.
2 Select three or four different shares and follow their prices over a period of months. Use graphs and note on them any reason(s) for major changes in the prices.
3 Explain the importance of the 'yield' in relation to shares.
4 Discuss the role of 'bulls' 'bears' and 'stags' on the Stock Market and how they affect share prices.
5 Describe the different types of securities which are traded on the Stock Market.

Assignment 13

Introduction

Assignment 13 is an exercise based on the main principles and types of insurance. It covers the importance of insurance in helping to minimise some of the risks in a business.

On completion of this assignment you should be able to:

1 describe the main principles of insurance;
2 explain the purposes of insurance documents;
3 appreciate the role of insurance in business and personal situations;
4 distinguish between insurable and uninsurable risks.

Background information

Many years ago, a trader who lost goods in a fire or shipwreck would simply lose everything. This had the effect of slowing down the expansion of trade because of the risks involved. Therefore, insurance developed as a way of protecting people against unexpected losses.

Insurance is based on the 'pooling of risks'. Everyone who takes out insurance pays a sum of money called a **premium** which goes into an insurance fund or 'pool'. Insured people who suffer a loss will make a claim for compensation which is paid out of this fund. Premiums are based on the risk involved. This is calculated by the insurance company from past statistics so that they know how likely it is that a particular risk may actually occur. The greater the risk the higher the premium.

Everybody who wishes to take out insurance cover must first fill in a **proposal form**. This gives the insurance company details about the risk to be insured. Once the risk has been accepted the company will issue a **policy** which is an agreement setting out what risks have been insured against and for how long.
There are two kinds of insurance cover:

- **Insurance** is cover against something which *might* happen, for example, a fire in the home, a car accident or medical expenses when we go on holiday abroad.
- **Assurance** is cover against something which *will* happen, for example, death.

Principles of insurance
All insurance is based upon three main principles:

- **Insurable interest**   That is, everyone who takes out insurance must be in a position to suffer a personal loss if the insured event occurs.
- **Utmost good faith**   All questions on the proposal form must be answered truthfully and all relevant facts which could affect the risk must be disclosed. The insurance company, for its part, must state the terms of cover in a clear, understandable way.
- **Indemnity**   You should not make a profit from insurance. The aim is to put you back in the same position as before, i.e. to indemnify you.

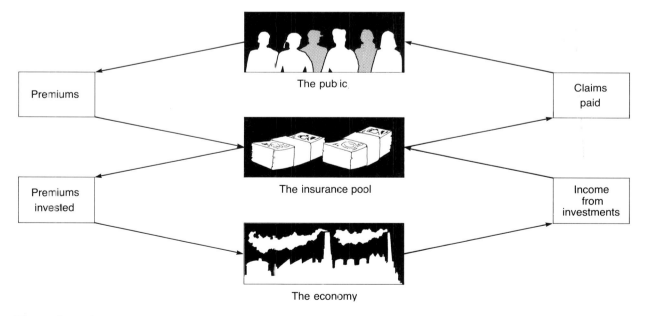

Premiums | The public | Claims paid
Premiums invested | The insurance pool | Income from investments
| The economy |

The pooling of risks

Business insurance

By law, a business must have employers' liability insurance to compensate staff who have accidents at work.
Other important types of business insurance include:

- **Buildings**   against fire or other damage
- **Goods in transit**   to cover the risks of theft or damage whilst goods are being delivered
- **Fidelity guarantee**   in case an employee steals money or goods from the firm

- **Motor vehicle**   by law, 'third party' insurance is necessary. This covers passengers or pedestrians injured in accidents
- **Machinery and equipment**   against fire, theft or damage
- **Consequential loss**   covers any loss of earnings in a business following a fire or other damage.
  Not all risks can be insured against. For example, a business cannot insure against making a trading loss or against goods going out of fashion because these risks cannot be calculated.

Business risks

Assignment

You are asked to complete the following tasks which are based on the background information provided.

Tasks

1 Insurance is described as 'the pooling of risks'. Explain what this means. (2)

2 The following sentences all relate to insurance. Complete each by selecting the appropriate word(s) from the box below. Use each answer *once* only. You do not have to use *every* possible answer.

a The application which a person completes and sends to the insurance company is called a
....

b The money paid for insurance is known as the
....

c An insurance .... is the contract which gives the terms and conditions in detail.

d You are allowed to insure your own house but not that of your neighbours. This illustrates the principle of ....

e The principle of .... means that you cannot make a profit out of a loss should the insured event occur.

f .... is the principle whereby all insurance contracts are dependent upon correct details being supplied otherwise the insurance company may refuse to pay any subsequent claim.

g Insurance against losses through the dishonesty of an employee is called a ....

h The difference between insurance and
.... is that the latter *will* happen
whilst the former *may* happen.

i .... insurance is compulsory for all
motor vehicle owners.

j The calculation of insurance premiums is based on
.... of past claims. (10)

> fidelity guarantee indemnity policy risk
> information proposal form third party
> premium loss fund assurance statistics
> utmost good faith pool insurable interest

3 Discuss whether or not Mr Patel has an insurable
interest in each of the following:

a the life of his wife Anita

b the contents of his house

c the life of his squash partner, John White

d the car bought specially for use in his business

e the business premises which he rents from the local
council. (10)

4 Explain why it would be sensible to insure each of the
following:

a a new car comprehensively

b jewellery worth £5,000

c a shop window

d the contents of a house situated alongside a river

e the life of a married man with two young children. (10)

5 Bill Smith owns a small clothing factory in the busy
market town of Upton. Bill employs ten staff in the
factory. He also owns two small vans and employs two
drivers for warehousing and delivery work.

a Explain to Bill why you think it is essential for any
business to take out insurance. (2)

b Identify six risks which you think Bill should insure
against in his business. (6)

c Choose two of the above six risks and give an
example of the type of information which the
insurance company will need in order to calculate the
premiums to be paid for each. (6)

d Name two risks which he cannot insure against.
Give reasons for your answer. (4)

Further development

The following ideas could be used to develop this
assignment.

1 Describe the different functions of insurance companies,
brokers and agents.

2 Invite a speaker from a local insurance organisation to
talk about the services they offer.

3 Discuss the importance of insurance to the economy,
and the benefits which it brings.

4 Collect examples of proposal forms from various
insurance companies and practise completing them.

Multiple choice 2

This section contains a series of questions or incomplete sentences followed by four possible responses. In each case select the most appropriate answer.

1 In a free enterprise economy the problem of what goods should be produced is decided by:
   a the government
   b the pattern of consumers' spending
   c the amount of advertising
   d what firms choose to produce.

2 The most important feature of a mixed economy is that:
   a resources are allocated in response to the profit motive;
   b there is government control of the production of goods and services;
   c each firm produces a mixture of goods and services;
   d goods and services are supplied by both private and state owned businesses.

3 Limited liability means that:
   a a firm cannot make a loss;
   b employees are insured against accidents at work;
   c shareholders cannot be asked to pay for a company's debts;
   d a firm is either a public or private company.

4 Which of the following is an example of a nationalised industry?
   a ICI
   b British Telecom
   c Marks and Spencer
   d British Coal

5 In law, a monopoly exists when a company controls what percentage of the total supply of a product?
   a 25%
   b 33.3%
   c 50%
   d 100%

6 Which of the following takeovers/mergers is *not* an example of horizontal integration?
   a Peugot–Talbot
   b Dixon's–Currys
   c British Airways–British Caledonian
   d Cadbury's–Schweppes

7 Which of the following is *not* an external economy of scale to a firm?
   a Supply of skilled labour
   b Local education and training provision
   c Installation of computerised equipment
   d Specialist delivery services

8 A multi-national company is best defined as a business which:
   a sells a wide range of similar products
   b controls a number of other companies
   c has branches throughout the UK
   d has divisions in more than one country.

9 All of the following are examples of a franchised business except:
   a Dyno-Rod
   b Prontaprint
   c Sainsbury's
   d Kentucky Fried Chicken.

10 Which of the following would provide the best measure of the relative size of firms in an industry?
   a Number of employees
   b Number of places of business
   c Profits
   d Turnover

11 A shop which specialises mainly in one type of merchandise and has more than ten branches is known as a:
   a multiple
   b supermarket
   c co-operative
   d department store.

12 The features of hypermarkets include all but which *one* of the following?
   a Out of town location
   b Limited range of goods
   c Plenty of car parking space
   d Competitive prices on all goods

13 Which of the following documents is *not* used in the formation of a limited company?
   a Memorandum of Association
   b Articles of Association
   c Certificate of Incorporation
   d Bill of Lading

14 An investor owns 1,000 shares in a company which have a nominal value of £1,000 and a market value of £1,500. If a 10 per cent dividend is declared the shareholder would receive:
   a £10
   b £50
   c £100
   d £150

15 Which of the following securities are *not* traded on the Stock Exchange?
   a Ordinary shares
   b Gilt-Edged securities
   c Preference shares
   d Unit trusts

16 The 'pooling of risk' means that:
   a insurance companies share risks with each other;
   b one insurance company re-insures with another;
   c those facing risks pay premiums which are used to compensate those suffering a loss;
   d the insured must personally be in a position to suffer loss should a misfortune occur.

17 Whilst a policy is being prepared an insurance company may accept the risk by issuing a:
   a proposal form
   b no claims bonus
   c cover note
   d claim form.

In each of the following questions, one or more of the responses is/are correct. Choose the appropriate letter which indicates the correct version.
   a if 1 only is correct.
   b if 3 only is correct.
   c if 1 and 2 only are correct.
   d if 1, 2 and 3 are correct.

18 Which of the following sources of capital are available to a partnership?
   1 Bank loans
   2 Retained profits
   3 Issue of shares

19 Which of the following reason(s) explain why small firms are able to survive?
   1 The size of some markets is limited.
   2 Service industries require local provision.
   3 Small specialist markets often exist.

20 Which of the following is/are a basic principle of insurance?
   1 Utmost good faith
   2 Indemnity
   3 Fidelity guarantee

D

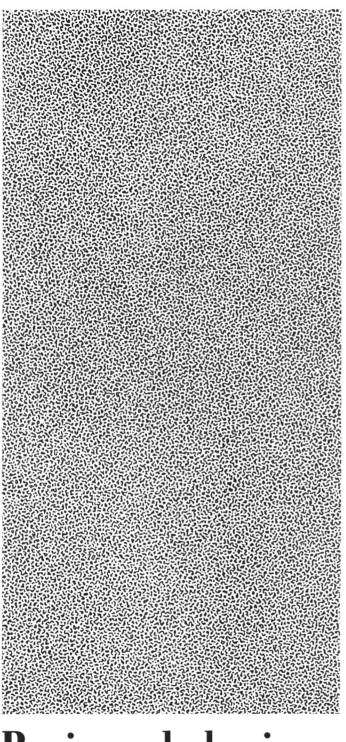

Business behaviour

Assignment 14

Market research survey

Introduction

Assignment 14 involves working in small groups to conduct a market reseach survey. Upon completion, each member of the group is asked to produce an individual report of the findings.

On completion of this assignment you should be able to:

1 understand the stages in a market research survey;
2 construct a market research questionnaire;
3 appreciate the importance of 'sampling';
4 use personal interviews to collect data;
5 analyse data and present it in the form of a report.

Background information

The term **marketing** is used to describe a whole group of business activities which are concerned with obtaining and keeping customers. Instead of firms saying, 'We only make two sizes of toothpaste (or carpet, or envelopes), take it or leave it!', they now ask customers, 'What type and size do you require?' The aim of good marketing is that firms should identify, by market research, the goods and services which consumers want and then produce them.

Street surveys and interviews are a popular way of finding out about the market

Market research involves collecting, recording and analysing information about products or markets. This could include information about consumers' sex, age, occupation, income, habits, likes and dislikes, where they live, which newspapers or magazines they read, and when they watch television. This information can be used to improve the way in which goods and services are marketed. A firm which finds out about the people who buy, or may buy, its products is far more likely to be successful in selling them.

Market research information can be obtained in two main ways:

Desk research, or secondary data, involves studying existing information. This may be the internal records of a firm, for example sales, stock, accounting records, customers' complaints, and salesmans' reports. It can also be obtained from information published by someone else, for example, newspapers, magazines or government journals such as the *Monthly Digest of Statistics*.

Field research involves the collection of primary or new information about a firm's products and markets, for example, by the use of questionnaires. A list of questions is drawn up and used to ask the opinions of existing or potential consumers by telephone, post or by interviewing in the street.

As it is impossible to contact everyone, market research surveys usually select a **sample** of people to answer questions. A sample is a cross-section of consumers differentiated by age, sex and occupation. The answers obtained from this sample should be very similar to asking everyone.

Random sampling

Using the information collected from market research, it is possible for firms to forecast (estimate) the likely sales of their products or services. To achieve these sales, important decisions have to be made based on the main activities involved in marketing, referred to as **the four 'P's**: product, price, promotion and place. Examples of the type of decisions involved are:

- **Product**   what and how much to produce
- **Price**   how much should be charged
- **Promotion**   where best to advertise and how to attract buyers
- **Place**   where to sell the products and how best to get them there.

Together these are known as the **marketing mix**.

51

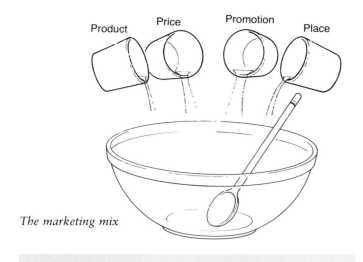

The marketing mix

Assignment

You are asked to carry out some research into an area of interest related to your school, college or place of work. This will give you practical experience of field research, including constructing a simple questionnaire, selecting and interviewing a sample, analysing the results and presenting them in the form of a short report.

Tasks

1 **Decide on the topic to be investigated**
   It could be why a particular product sells well, or what people think about your school/college/works magazine/newsletter, meals service or working conditions.

2 **Design a questionnaire**
   a *Information required.* It is necessary to decide what questions you want to ask, and then to write them

---

Crisp Survey   * Circle the answer

1 When did you last buy a packet of crisps?
   * Today   * Yesterday   * Within the last week
   * Within the last month   * Over a month ago

2 Which brand of crisps did you buy? . . . .

3 Why did you buy that particular brand? . . . .

4 Which flavour did you buy? . . . .

5 How did you rate the taste of the crisps?
   * Very good   * Good   * Fair   * Not very good
   * Poor

6 Would you buy the same brand again?   * Yes/No

7 Would you buy the same flavour again?   * Yes/No

8 What is your favourite flavour of crisp? . . . .

---

carefully in a clear and logical way. (It is recommended that your questionnaire is fairly brief, consisting of not more than 10–15 questions.)
   b *Question content.* It is possible to use different styles of questions. The following examples illustrate questions which require a simple *yes* or *no* response, those which give a choice of answers and those which leave the answer open-ended.

   Select a sample
   a When your questionnaire is ready the next task is to select the type and number of people that you wish to interview. For example, if you are attending a school with 1,000 pupils then you might decide to ask the opinions of 1 in every 20 pupils, i.e. 50 altogether. You could break this sample down further into various categories by interviewing 25 male and 25 female pupils and by dividing these into different age groups. Remember, if your sample is to be representative of all of the pupils you will need to select the people you interview very carefully.
   b You will need to reproduce sufficient copies (and spares) of your questionnaire to cover the total number required.

4 **Carry out the interviewing**
   Once the sample has been selected you can begin the interviews. If it is a group assignment, each person should interview a small number of people, perhaps ten.

5 **Analyse the results**
   Again, working as a group, it will be necessary to count the answers to each question. When completed, the results can be presented in the form of tables, charts and diagrams. These are often much easier to understand than a long written description.

6 **Present a report**
   Each group member should now present their own report of the survey. This should contain full details of each person's contribution to the assignment in addition to a summary of the work of the other group members. It should also give details of the problems involved in carrying out the research.
   A suitable structure might be as follows:
   a Title and purpose of report
   b Introduction
   c Body of report, i.e. presentation and analysis of data collected
   d Summary of findings including the value of the information discovered
   e Any conclusions or recommendations based on the findings.   (50)

Further development

The following ideas could be used to develop this assignment.

1 Invite speakers from a market research agency to talk about their work.
2 It is useful to have a class discussion based on the findings/limitations of the research and what changes could be made to improve the reliability of the survey.

Assignment 15

Cadbury's Dairy Milk

Introduction

Assignment 15 is a marketing case study about the problems caused by the product life cycle. It illustrates the importance of market research, product planning, advertising and sales promotion in a business.

On completion of this assignment you should be able to:

1 identify key information from the data provided;
2 outline how Cadbury's solved the Dairy Milk marketing problem;
3 explain a variety of terms and expressions used in marketing;
4 appreciate the importance of marketing in a business.

Background information

Just as we are born, grow up, mature and eventually become old and die, so the sales of many products have a similar life cycle. As the diagram shows, this **product life cycle** involves a number of important stages.

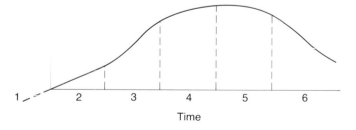

Stages in the product life cycle

1 **Development**   With the help of market research new products are designed.
2 **Introduction**   Once it has been developed, the product is advertised and brought to the market for sale.
3 **Growth**   If the product is successful sales will increase rapidly.

4 **Maturity**   Once established in a market, the sales of a product do not grow so rapidly. One main reason for this is likely to be increased competition as other firms introduce similar products.
5 **Saturation**   In time sales stop increasing.
6 **Decline**   Eventually competition and other new products are likely to result in falling sales and profits. If this continues the product may disappear from the market.

It was this last stage of the product life cycle which Cadbury's Dairy Milk was experiencing by 1980. First produced over 80 years ago, it had always been Cadbury's most important product. Until the late 1970s it was the market leader in moulded (i.e. solid) bar chocolate with over 40 per cent of total sales.

However, at this time, new brands like Galaxy and Yorkie were introduced in direct competition, and consumer tastes were also changing. Dairy Milk was not as thick and chunky as its competitors and this resulted in a sharp fall in sales. Faced with this problem, the company decided to find out what was wrong and then took action to put it right.

Assignment

You are asked to read through the advertisement on the next page, which gives details of what happened to Dairy Milk, and complete the tasks which relate to it. All answers or information given should be written in your own words.

Tasks

1 Name the three giant manufacturers who dominate the UK chocolate market. (3)
2 Why did Dairy Milk's share of the moulded chocolate bar sector fall from 42.8 per cent to 37.1 per cent between 1970 and 1980? (3)
3 From years of research, Cadbury's were able to find out that people thought that theirs was the 'definitive' chocolate, i.e. the original and the best. What did the public think about other brands of chocolate? (1)
4 What did the company do to recover Dairy Milk's popularity? Give three examples. (4)
5 How much money was spent on the major advertising campaign and what was the theme which was used? (2)
6 Give two examples of the savings which the company made by introducing the new manufacturing processes. (4)

In the battle for the heart of the chocolate market, Cadbury Schweppes management stuck it out through thin and thick.

Cadbury's Dairy Milk Chocolate is one of the few products which has probably been enjoyed by most people in the country, at one time or another. It is almost as old as the century, and the fact that every ½lb contains a glass and a half of full cream dairy milk is something we've all known since birth, or so it seems.

Yet no brand, no matter how well loved and established is invulnerable. By the late 1970's the Dairy Milk brand ran into a few problems.

The fact that the problems were solved and competitive attacks were fought off successfully, enabling the brand to emerge as marketing's most vigorous 81 year old, is a tale of determined management.

Here's what happened:

Award yourself 42% of the market.

The U.K. chocolate market is huge, worth more than £1.9 billion at retail selling price. It has traditionally been dominated by three giant manufacturers, Cadbury, Mars and Rowntree. The market has a number of subdivisions. Dairy Milk is in the moulded bar sector and ten years ago held a 42.8% share.

Despite this seemingly healthy position a number of factors were coinciding to put pressure on Dairy Milk.

The moulded chocolate sector was in a long-term decline compared to the countline (filled bars) sector due in part to a lack of investment and changing consumer tastes.

The Dairy Milk product had undergone changes. In order to keep the surface area to a familiar size while simultaneously keeping the bar affordable, the product lost one of its prime characteristics – chunkiness.

And to cap it all there was the successful launch of a directly competitive product.

All this resulted in a 1980 market share of 37.1%.

Chocolate is Cadbury's.

It was crucial, for business and emotional reasons, that Cadbury should get Dairy Milk back into the heart of the market.

There was an underlying public belief about the brand revealed by years of research, that Cadbury's was the definitive chocolate with other brands being mere imitations. That was the position to be recovered as soon as possible.

And it was recovered, by the application of one of the most easily overlooked of the 'management skills' – a ruthless degree of thoroughness, applied to every aspect of both product and marketplace.

A bigger chunk (of money).

The first move was to make Dairy Milk as chunky and mouth-filling as it ever had been. Making the bar break with a satisfying crack was a move which has endeared the product to the British public.

£50 million was then spent making the Dairy Milk manufacturing process the most modern in Europe.

Speed of production has been increased tenfold by microprocessor control. The wrapping machine speeds have been more than doubled, so the number of machines could be halved. Output per employee is up 25% while the number of moulding plants has dropped from 21 to 4.

This meant Cadbury could produce a product of great quality and consistency. It also gave Cadbury the financial capability to spend another £3.5 million on advertising.

This is Cadbury.

That was the theme of the major advertising campaign Cadbury commissioned to re-establish its chocolate values.

This was linked with a re-design of the pack, which made it more salient and more 'Cadbury' in appearance. Then maximum trade penetration was achieved by dint of heroic work by the sales force. Dairy Milk is a 'must stock' item in every type of possible confectionery outlet. Vital in a market where it's estimated that 70% of purchases are made on impulse.

This is success...

It all worked. The moulded sector of the chocolate market is no longer in decline.

Dairy Milk's share of that market has made a steady and sustained recovery. By 1985 it was at 43.3% and had overtaken its 1976 position.

By 1985, the chunky 60g pack of Dairy Milk had recovered to the point where sales were double those of the nearest competitor when measured in consumer sales.

There has been an even bigger success with the key family block market, where the 200g block of Dairy Milk outsells its two major competitors combined. *By more than double.*

...and a half.

Dairy Milk is now back in its rightful position as brand leader of the moulded sector, stronger than ever before.

The effective management of the Dairy Milk brand has also had a considerable rub-off effect on brands like Wholenut and Fruit and Nut, both of which are going from strength to strength.

What's more, this continual process of anticipating and responding to consumer tastes is, of course, what effective brand management is all about.

A brand such as Dairy Milk, with all its history and heritage, can be fine tuned in order to ensure relevance to today's consumers, and indeed tomorrow's.

As Neville Bain, Managing Director of Cadbury Limited, says: "Dairy Milk has always been the flagship brand of our company. The highly successful and profitable turnaround of the brand is indicative of the determination and thoroughness of our entire management team."

Cadbury Schweppes

MANAGEMENT PROVEN IN THE MARKET PLACE

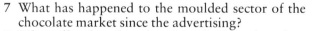

---

7 What has happened to the moulded sector of the chocolate market since the advertising? *(1)*

8 What effect has the advertising had on the sales of Dairy Milk? *(4)*

9 Explain, with examples, what is meant by each of the following marketing terms. These have all been highlighted in the text.

a Brand
b UK chocolate market
c Changing consumer tastes
d Directly competitive product
e Trade penetration
f Impulse purchases
g Brand leader
h Brand management
i 'Rub-off effect'
j Flagship brand *(20)*

10 Most bars of chocolate are available in several different sizes. Suggest reasons for this based on your own experience. *(8)*

Further development

The following ideas could be used to develop this assignment.

1 Arrange a visit to a chocolate manufacturer.
2 Conduct a survey of the chocolate consumption of your group. This could be carried out along the lines suggested in Assignment 14.
3 In small groups, carry out a study of the way in which the three major chocolate manufacturers advertise and promote their products. In particular, look at television, newspaper and magazine advertising. How does this change at different times of the year to reflect seasonal demands like Easter and Christmas?

Assignment 16

Introduction

Assignment 16 is a study of advertising and its importance to businesses. It consists of a series of exercises which provide information to help you to solve a case study problem. You can tackle it working individually or in groups.

On completion of this assignment you should be able to:

1 describe how and why firms advertise;
2 identify different methods of advertising;

Why advertise?

3 understand the importance of effective advertising and sales promotion;
4 apply your knowledge to solve a business problem.

Background information

An important part of marketing is called **sales promotion**. This involves all the activities used by businesses to maintain and increase their sales. Customers must be made aware of what a firm has to sell and then be persuaded to buy it. Advertising is the chief means of sales promotion.

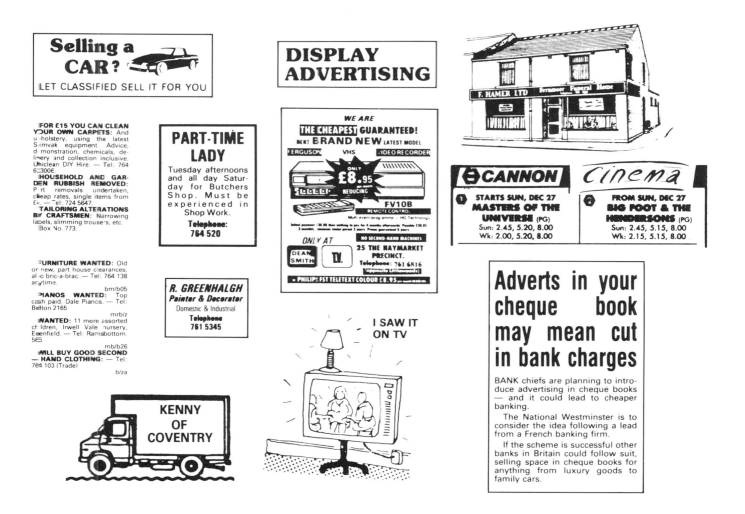

Advertising media

Methods of advertising include the following:

- **Press** newspapers and magazines which can be local or national.
- **Television** local or national.
- **Radio** local or Luxemburg
- **Outdoor** hoardings, posters and neon signs.

} These are called **mass media** because they can reach millions of people everywhere.

- **Direct mail** catalogues, circulars and leaflets through the post.
- **Sponsorship** for example, of sporting events or players, such as the Football League by Barclays Bank.

Advertisements also appear on carrier bags, key rings, pens, the cinema screen and in Yellow Pages.

The **cost of advertising** depends on the media used and the size or length of the advertisement. A firm wanting to advertise will consider not just the cost involved, but also the type of goods or services being promoted, the budget it has to spend. the market it is trying to reach and the results expected. The aim is to find the most effective media at the lowest cost.

Firms can either arrange their own advertising or use an advertising agency. Advertising agencies are specialist firms who will plan and carry out an advertising campaign for which they charge a fee.

Control of Advertising
There is careful control of what can be said or shown in advertisements. This consists of:

- **Voluntary Control** by the firms in the advertising industry for example, by following the 'British Code of Advertising Practice'. This aims to make advertising 'legal, decent, honest and truthful'.
- **Legal Controls** such as the Trade Descriptions Act, 1968 and the Consumer Credit Act, 1974.

Other methods of Sales Promotion
- **Price reductions** for example, annual sales and special offers
- **Trading stamps** for example, Green Shield, Co-op
- **'Loss leaders'** selling items at below cost to attract customers.
- **Personality promotions** for example, using a television star to open a shop or exhibition.
- **Free gifts** for example free plugs with irons, or pillows with beds
- **Exhibitions and Trade Fairs** for example, The Motor Show and Boat Show
- **Coupons** for example, 10p off the next purchase
- **Competitions** for example, holidays and cars as prizes

Branded Goods
Most goods are given 'brand names', for example Heinz, Sony and Farah. Branding makes large scale advertising effective because potential customers can be persuaded to ask for products by name.

Shopping by post?
Play it safe
Look for the initials
MOPS

For full details send a 9" x 6"
stamped addressed envelope to:
The National Newspaper
Mail Order Protection Scheme
16 Tooks Court, London EC4A 1LB

Advertisements are expected to conform to rules and standards laid down by the Advertising Standards Authority. Most do. The few that don't we'd like you to write in about.

And if you'd like a copy of these rules for press, poster and cinema advertisements, please send for our booklet. It's free.

The Advertising Standards Authority.
We're here to put it right. ✓

ASA Ltd., Dept. C, Brook House, Torrington Place, London WC1E 7HN.

Some methods of sales promotion

Assignment

Carefully read the background information and then complete the following tasks.

Tasks

1 Explain why firms advertise. (2)
2 Using examples, explain why branding is important for advertising. (3)
3 Name ten different advertising media. (5)
4 Outline the main factors which a business should consider when choosing advertising media. (6)
5 Say which method(s) of advertising and promotion you consider to be the most suitable and effective for each of the following. Be specific and give reasons for your answer.

   a A small local newsagent
   b A multiple shoe retailer
   c A large mail order company
   d A bank
   e A teenage magazine
   f To attract foreign tourists to your area
   g To introduce a new toothpaste
   h To sell a second-hand bicycle
   i To promote a school charity concert
   j To sell Rolls-Royce cars (10)

6 a Advertisements in the press can be either 'classified' or 'display'. Find two examples of each and discuss the ways in which they are different. (3)
   b Collect three press advertisements aimed at teenagers. Give your opinion of each saying whether or not you feel they are likely to be effective. Give reasons for your conclusions. (3)
7 Devise advertisements, suitable for two different media, to encourage parents to send their children to your school/college or place of work. (6)
8 Use some of the information in Tasks 1–7 to help you in considering the following problem.

Imagine that you work in a local grocery store. The store has a reputation for quality goods and service, although its prices are often considered to be rather high.

The turnover in the store has been falling off rapidly in recent weeks following the opening of a nearby hypermarket. The owners have stated that they must see an improvement in sales within the next month or the store may be forced to close down.

Your task is to consider what can be done to prevent the closure. (12)

Further development

The following ideas can be used to develop this assignment.
1 Carry out a study into the cost of advertising in different media.
2 Consider the arguments for and against advertising.
3 Make a list of advertisements shown on television and make a note of the number of times they are shown in one evening (or within a particular period of time). Consider:
   a the age group or type of person at which each is aimed;
   b whether they are of national, or purely local interest;
   c what gimmick, if any, is used to catch people's attention;
   d any other interesting features;
   e what conclusions can you draw from your findings?

Assignment 17

You want it when?

Introduction

Assignment 17 is a case study based on the problems which a firm can face in distributing its products to its customers. It illustrates the importance of the correct choice of transport and how this can affect a company's reputation and marketing.

On completion of this assignment you should be able to:

1 describe the main features of private limited companies;
2 explain the use of containers in transport;
3 identify a firm's distribution problems;
4 outline the advantages and disadvantages of different types of transport;
5 understand the reasons for a particular choice of transport.

Background information

The importance of transport
Transport is concerned with the movement of materials, goods or people from one place to another and is therefore an essential part of marketing and trade.

- **Raw materials** must be transported to factories, often between one country and another.
- **Goods** need to be distributed from factories to wholesalers, retailers and consumers.
- **People** must be transported both to and from work and also for leisure and other activities like shopping and holidays.

An efficient transport system is essential to enable trade to take place throughout the world and to improve standards of living.

The importance of transport

Choice of transport
A business has a choice of using road, rail, sea or air transport. However, not all methods are suitable for the movement of all freight (goods and materials). Therefore, the form of transport used by any business will depend upon the relative importance of a number of factors including the type of goods, their value, size and weight, the cost, speed, frequency and convenience of the method of transport and the distance involved.

Types of transport
- In the UK, most inland transport of goods and people takes place by **road**, the main advantage of which is its door to door service over a wide area.
- The **railways** are particularly suited to moving large quantities of bulk freight over long distances.
- **Inland waterways** (rivers and canals) are a slow but relatively cheap means of transport available only on limited routes.
- **Sea** transport is very important for the import and export of goods. This method of transport is slow but cheap, and provides access to countries throughout the world.
- **Air freight** traffic is growing steadily and provides the quickest means of means of transport particularly over long distances.

Hovercrafts on cross-channel routes and **pipelines** in the North Sea are examples of other types of transport, whilst some future developments could include wider use of electric vehicles, conveyor belts, hovertrains, vertical take-off and landing aircraft, monorails and the building of the Channel Tunnel.

A BP oil refinery at Grangemouth

Containers

Probably the most important development in recent years in the field of freight transport has been the introduction of containers. These are large metal cases into which goods are packed at the factory and delivered directly to their destination as a unit load. The containers are transported by lorries and transferred by special cranes onto trains or ships. This makes the transport of goods much cheaper, safer and more efficient.

Containers are designed to be easy to transport

Assignment

Read the situation below and complete the tasks that follow.

Homefit Kitchens is a small but growing private limited company which manufactures and supplies 'tailor made' kitchen units. The firm is located in the North of England within easy reach of the M6 and M61 motorways and the Inter-City rail network. It has regional offices in Manchester, Birmingham and London with a team of sales representatives based in each. The company has recently decided to sell a range of consumer durables including cookers, refrigerators and washing machines. It has negotiated a special price contract with a major manufacturer but must buy goods by the container load. Homefit sells direct to its customers and this would mean that it could now supply them with a complete kitchen. It plans to store the goods by building an extension to its existing warehouse.

At present all goods are collected from the factory and delivered by Swift Transport, a firm of outside contractors. Swift's service has been generally good. However, recently there have been a number of problems: there have been some delays in delivery, some items have been delivered damaged and there have also been a number of incorrect deliveries. Homefit accept that some, but not all, of this is the company's fault, caused by out of stock items, poor packaging and incorrect addresses.

Distribution Manager, Ian O'Leary, would like the firm to introduce its own fleet of vehicles. He believes that this would increase efficiency. He has the support of John McCathy, the Marketing Manager, who is worried about possible damage to the present advertising campaign based on the slogan 'Buy Homefit for guaranteed quality, style and fast delivery'. John believes that the high initial investment will produce considerable long-term benefits for the company.

However, Managing Director, Ken Ferguson, remains unconvinced and at a recent Board Meeting made the following statement:

Road haulage offers many advantages to us as a company and we cannot seriously consider any other form of transport. It is a very competitive business so I cannot see how we can justify the costs of introducing our own fleet of delivery vehicles.

Tasks

1 Homefit is a private limited company. Describe the main features of such companies. (3)
2 What benefits, if any, does the company have from being situated within easy reach of the Inter-City rail network? (3)
3 a Explain what you understand by the term 'consumer durables'. (1)
  b Suggest two other kitchen appliances which Homefit might decide to offer to its customers. (2)
4 a How are Homefit kitchens sold to the public? (1)
  b How are they delivered? (1)
5 What problems will Homefit face when it starts to sell consumer durables? (4)
6 a What are containers? (1)
  b Why do you think the company is being asked to buy the consumer durables by the container load? (4)
7 a Why is the company currently concerned about its delivery to customers? (4)
  b In what ways is it the company's fault? (3)
8 a What advantages does road transport offer to the company? (4)
  b Why does Ken Ferguson say that it is not possible for Homefit to consider other forms of transport? (2)
9 What did the Managing Director mean when he said that road haulage 'is a very competitive business'? (2)
10 a Do you think Homefit should continue to use outside carriers or would it be a better policy for the company to introduce its own transport fleet? Give reasons for your choice. (10)
  b What else could the company do instead of buying its own vehicles? (5)

Further development

The following ideas could be used to develop this assignment.

1 Compare the transport services provided in the public sector with those provided in the private sector.
2 Discuss the reasons for the growth of air transport and explain why it is unsuitable for some types of freight.
3 Describe the advantages and disadvantages for a firm that is considering using sea transport. Outline the main documents which would be necessary for transporting goods in this way.

Assignment 18

Business documents

Introduction

Assignment 18 is a series of exercises based on the main business documents. It is designed to be completed individually.

On completion of this assignment you should be able to:

1 explain the main documents used in a business transaction;
2 calculate the cost of an order;
3 appreciate the difference between trade and cash discount.

Background information

The buying and selling of goods is called a **transaction**. This often involves considerable paperwork. Therefore, special **documents** are frequently used in order to make the process as quick and efficient as possible. They provide a record of each transaction and make communication easier. Each of these documents has a particular purpose in passing information between buyers and sellers and although they may vary from firm to firm, the basic principles are the same.

In a typical business transaction some or all of the following documents could be used:

- **Enquiry**
  When a business wishes to buy goods it will frequently make an enquiry to several firms asking them if they can supply the goods. It will also ask for details of the price, quality and delivery dates. This enquiry may take the form of a letter or a standard printed form.
- **Quotation**
  In reply, the firms approached will send a letter, catalogue or price list. This will quote details of the price, delivery and any terms such as Trade and Cash Discount.
- **Estimate**
  Where no standard prices exist, a firm usually sends an estimate of how much the goods are likely to cost.
- **Order**
  When a firm decides to purchase goods it will place an order.
- **Acknowledgement of order**
  Many firms will confirm an order by writing to say that it is receiving attention.
- **Advice note**
  This is sometimes sent to tell a customer that the goods are on the way.

A delivery note is signed on receipt of goods

- **Delivery** or **despatch note**
  Goods sent in the suppliers *own* vehicle are usually accompanied by a delivery note. The customer can use this to check that they have received what was ordered.
- **Consignment note**
  This is used when a firm does not deliver goods itself but sends them by road or rail transport.
- **Invoice**
  An invoice is sent by the supplier to the customer when goods have been bought on credit. It includes a description of the goods, the quantity supplied, the price charged and the total cost.
- **Pro forma invoice**
  This is similar to an invoice but is not charged to a customer's account. They are often used when goods have already been paid for, or are sent on approval or sale or return. Mail order catalogue firms use this type of invoice.
- **Statement of account**
  This is a request for payment of a customer's account and is usually sent monthly. It includes details of that month's invoices plus any credit or debit notes. The balance at the end is the amount owed.
- **Credit note**
  A credit note is sent to a customer to correct an overcharge or to give a refund, for example, when faulty or damaged goods are returned. It has the effect of reducing the amount owed.

- **Debit note**
  A debit note is sent to correct an undercharge, for example, when a mistake has been made on an invoice. It has the effect of increasing the amount owed.
- **Value Added Tax (VAT)**
  VAT is a tax by the government on sales and is usually added to the selling price of most goods and services. Therefore, a trader may well add VAT to an invoice thus increasing the cost of the goods purchased. The current rate of VAT is 15%.

Assignment

Having read the background information you are asked to complete the following tasks.

Tasks

1 Copy and complete the flow chart by filling in the words from the list below in the correct order. (8)

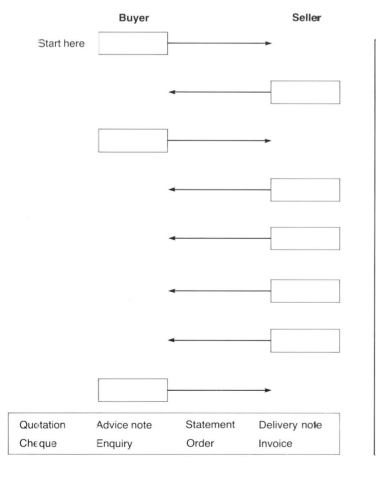

| Quotation | Advice note | Statement | Delivery note |
| Cheque | Enquiry | Order | Invoice |

2 Match the documents in List A with the correct definition in List B. Use each letter once only. You do not have to use every definition.

List A Documents	List B Definitions
1 Advice note	a Used when goods are sent on approval
2 Statement of account	b A request to a firm asking them to supply goods
3 Order	c Summary of a customer's transactions with the selling firm
4 Debit note	d Used when goods are delivered in a firm's own vehicle
5 Pro forma invoice	e Used when goods are damaged and/or returned
	f Is sent to rectify an undercharge
	g Informs the buyer that goods are being delivered

(5)

Tasks 3–5 are based on a transaction between S. Bray and Quick Fit Ltd. For each calculation, show how you worked out your answer.

3 From the following order, complete the invoice No. 123 dated 15 July 1988. VAT at 15 per cent is applicable to all the goods which are subject to 20 per cent Trade Discount. A further 5 per cent Cash Discount is offered if the invoice is paid within one month.
Calculate the total cost of the goods ordered. (15)

ORDER

HEATING PLUMBING SERVICES

Quick Fix Ltd
12 Silver Road
CROYDON

To: S. Bray (Plumbers' Merchants)
17 Farwood Road
GUILDFORD

No: 251
10 July 1988

PLEASE SUPPLY THE FOLLOWING GOODS

Cat. No.	Quantity	Details	Unit Price
4/34	20 metres	Copper pipe 22 mm	£1.79
5/38	100 tins	Putty	0.60
30/46	4	Radiators 950 mm single	£22.80
3/94	2	Central Heating Boilers 40,000 BTU	£295.90

INVOICE

HEATING PLUMBING SERVICES

TO:

Date

Your Order No.

VAT Registration No.

197476323

Cat. No.	Quantity	Description	Unit Price £	Total Price £
			15% VAT	£

Terms:
E and O E

---

4 One of the central heating boilers was returned by S. Bray because it was faulty.
  a What is the name of the document which Quick Fix Ltd would send to S. Bray? (2)
  b What will be the amount shown on the document? (8)
5 On 31 July, Quick Fix Ltd sent a statement to S. Bray. Invoice No. 123 and the document in Task 4 were the only items shown on the statement.
  a Calculate the balance owing on 31 July. (6)
  b S. Bray paid his account by cheque on 18 August 1988. How much did he pay? (6)

Further development

The following ideas could be used to develop this assignment.

1 Contact a local business and ask to see copies of its business documents.
2 Design your own logo and set of business documents. Include on them any appropriate terms or special conditions and explain the reasons for the designs you have used.
3 Practise completing business documents.

Assignment 19

Murphy's break-even

Introduction

Assignment 19 is a problem solving exercise based on the break-even point of a firm. It considers the relationship between the costs which a firm faces and the level of output and sales necessary before it can make a profit.

Or completion of this assignment you should be able to:

1 describe the main functions of a company's directors;
2 distinguish between fixed and variable costs;
3 appreciate how average costs change with the volume of production;
4 explain the importance of the break-even point;
5 understand the relationship between costs, output and sales.

Background information

Most businesses exist to make a **profit** which they achieve by supplying goods and services to satisfy people's needs and wants. In order to make a profit a firm will buy or make goods at one price and sell them at a higher price, thus profit is the difference between the sales revenue and the costs.

Businesses incur two types of costs: fixed costs and variable costs. **Fixed costs**, or overheads, are those which must be paid whether a firm produces anything or not. Examples of fixed costs would be: rent for premises, heating, lighting and insurance. They do not vary in the short-term. **Variable costs**, on the other hand, vary directly with output. For example, if a firm produces more, it will need additional raw materials, labour and transport and therefore its variable costs will increase.

As a firm sells more so the **average cost** of producing each unit will fall. This is because the fixed costs do not change and are therefore spread over a larger output.

$$\text{Average cost} = \frac{\text{Total cost}}{\text{Output}} \text{ (Fixed and variable costs)}$$

To avoid making a loss a firm needs to know how many articles must be sold at a given price to cover its costs. If a firm makes neither a profit nor a loss, it is said to **break-even**.

Output	Fixed costs	Variable costs	Total costs	Average total costs	Sales revenue
	£	£	£	£	£
0	180	0	180	180	0
1	180	50	230	230	110
2	180	100	280	140	220
3	180	150	330	110	330*
4	180	200	380	95	440
5	180	250	430	85	550
6	180	300	480	80	660

The table shows a firm with fixed costs of £180 per unit, variable costs of £50 per unit and a selling price of £110. In this situation the firm would need to sell three units before it reaches the break-even point*. Beyond this point, total sales revenue exceeds total costs and therefore the firm makes a profit. However, if the firm sells less than three units it will be operating at a loss.

A firm's break-even point occurs when its total costs equal its total sales revenue. This relationship between a firm's output, costs and sales can also be shown on a break-even chart.

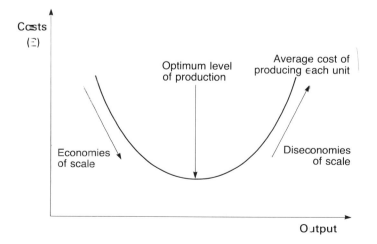

Costs of production

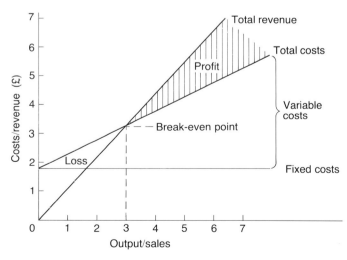

Break-even chart

E

The break-even point can also be calculated using the following formula:

$$\text{Break-even} = \frac{F}{S-V}$$

where F = Fixed costs
S = Selling price
V = Variable costs

Thus in the table on page 59

F = £180   S = £110   V = £50

Therefore break-even = $\dfrac{180}{110-50}$ = 3 units

Break-even analysis is used by businesses because it enables them to assess the effect on profits of changes in costs, price or turnover. However, it assumes that all goods produced are sold and that costs and selling price remain constant; this may be unrealistic.

Assignment

Read the situation described below and complete the tasks that follow.

Murphy Enterprises Ltd is a manufacturer of high quality wooden doors which it supplies mainly to the building trade. Currently the company produces 4,500 doors per year which it sells for £100 each. Fixed costs are £165,000 per annum and variable costs £45 per door.

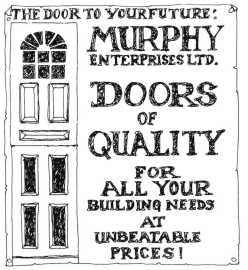

At a recent meeting of the board of directors, managing director Alistair Peart said that the company must improve its present output and profits. Marketing director Mike Scanlon stated that he believed that the company could increase its current

selling price by 10 per cent and still remain competitive. Production director Joe Bennett estimated that to double current production would increase the firm's variable costs by a third although fixed costs should remain the same.

The directors feel that before reaching a final decision they would like to see some break-even details at the next meeting.

Tasks

1 Is Murphy's a public or private limited company? How can you tell from the information provided? (2)
2 a What is a 'board of directors'? (2)
   b Briefly describe the main functions of the managing director in a company? (2)
   c Name two other directors who might be on the Board at Murphy's and outline their likely responsibilities. (4)
3 a With the use of examples, explain the term 'fixed costs'. (2)
   b What are the company's current fixed costs? (1)
4 a With the use of examples, explain the term 'variable costs'. (2)
   b What are the company's current variable costs per door? (1)
5 Calculate the following for the current year:
   a Total variable costs (2)
   b Total costs (2)
   c Total revenue (2)
   d The average cost of producing:
      500 doors
      4,000 doors (4)
6 a Draw a break-even chart and show on it Murphy's current break-even point. (4)
   b What is the break-even output? (2)
7 Assuming that the company achieves its revised targets, calculate the new break-even point. (2)
8 a What is Murphy's new sales target? (2)
   b Suggest reasons why the firm might not achieve its sales targets at the new selling price. (2)
   c What action could the firm take if sales do not meet their target? (6)
   d Advise the company whether, in your opinion, it should go ahead with the proposed new production and pricing structures. (6)

Further development

The following ideas could be used to develop this assignment.

1 Discuss the ways in which Murphy's could reduce its fixed and variable costs, for example, by introducing new technology.
2 Identify the fixed and variable costs in your school, college or place of work.
3 Consider the effect of the market forces of supply and demand on a firm's break-even point.

Assignment 20

Ritetime's final accounts

Introduction

Assignment 20 is an individual exercise based on a company's final accounts. It illustrates the importance of keeping accounting records and shows how a simple profit and loss account, and balance sheet can be used to assess the financial performance of a business.

On completion of this assignment you should be able to:

1 distinguish between gross and net profit;
2 distinguish between assets and liabilities;
3 extract information from a balance sheet;
4 explain the importance of working capital;
5 use simple ratios to analyse a firm's final accounts.

Background information

At the end of each financial year, any business needs to know whether or not it has made a profit. To provide this information, accounting records are kept from which final accounts are prepared. Profits represent the return (reward) for the risks taken in setting up and running a business. A **Trading and Profit Loss Account** is drawn up to show the gross and net profit (or loss) for the year. **Gross profit** is the difference between the cost of purchasing raw materials or goods and the selling price. From this figure, the costs of running the business (such as rent and wages) are deducted to find the **net profit**. These accounts are prepared to help control the business.

Stock, an asset, is usually stored in a warehouse

The overall financial position of the business is shown on a **balance sheet**. This shows how much money has been put into a business and how it has been spent. It has two sides, which are equal to each other, consisting of **assets** (what is owned by the business) and **liabilities** (anything owed by the business).

Assets which remain the same over a period of time such as buildings, equipment and furniture are called **fixed assets**. Each year some of these assets will lose value due to wear and tear. Therefore in its accounts a business will make an allowance for this called **depreciation**. This can eventually be used to replace them. Assets which change from day to day such as stock and cash are called **current assets**.

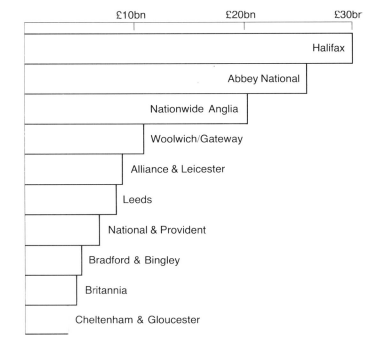

Building societies' assets in 1987

Liabilities are are also of two types: **fixed liabilities**, such as capital and long-term loans which remain the same over long periods, and **current** liabilities such as creditors, bank overdrafts and short-term loans which change from day to day.

By subtracting the current liabilities from the current assets we can find the **working capital**. This is the money which a firm needs to meet its day to day expenses such as wages and the purchasing of stock.

Working capital is essential to enable a firm to operate efficiently and remain solvent, that is, in a position to pay its expenses. If a business is insolvent it means that the current assets are less than the current liabilities and thus it cannot pay its debts in full. If this continues for any length of time the business may be forced to cease trading.

By examining the accounts it is possible to discover the financial strengths and weaknesses of a business. The following performance measures are some of those used and often form the basis of future planning decisions.

1 | **Average stock:** $\dfrac{\text{Opening stock} + \text{Closing stock}}{2}$

This shows how much money the business has 'tied-up' in stock.

2 | **Rate of Turnover**

$\dfrac{\text{Total sales}}{\text{Average stock at selling price}}$

Or

$\dfrac{\text{Cost of goods sold}}{\text{Average stock at cost price}}$

Either formula can be used to show how often a business is selling its stock. The second formula is usually simpler to apply.

3 | **Profit on Turnover:** $\dfrac{\text{Gross profit}}{\text{Turnover}} \times 100 = \%$

Or

$\dfrac{\text{Net profit}}{\text{Turnover}} \times 100 = \%$

This gives a percentage profit figure which can be used for comparison with previous years and the profits of other businesses.

4 | **Return on Capital:**

$\dfrac{\text{Net profit}}{\text{Total assets} - \text{Current liabilities}} \times 100 = \%$

This gives the yield or return on capital which provides a comparison with previous years and with other forms of investment.

Assignment

Having read the background information study the following extract from the accounts of Ritetime Watch Co Ltd and complete the tasks that follow.

Trading and Profit and Loss Account For the year ending 30 September			
	£		£
Opening stock	20,000	Turnover	220,000
Cost of goods sold	160,000	Closing stock	12,000
Gross profit	52,000		
	232,000		232,000
Expenses	24,500	Gross profit	52,000
Net profit	27,500		
	52,000		52,000

Balance Sheet as at 30 September				
	£			£
Authorised Capital		Premises		20,000
40,000 £1		Equipment	18,500	
Ordinary shares	40,000	Less depreciation	2,000	
				16,500
Issued Capital		Vehicles	5,800	
35,000 £1		Less depreciation	800	5,000
Ordinary shares	35,000	Stock		10,200
10% Debentures	5,000	Debtors		4,200
Reserves	6,500	Bank		1,800
Short-term bank		Cash		1,500
loan	8,500			
Creditors	2,000			
Overdraft	2,200			
	59,200			59,200

Tasks

1 To what type of business organisation do the above figures relate? (1)
2 What is the purpose of the profit and loss account? (2)
3 Explain the terms:
  a Gross profit (2)
  b Net profit (2)
  c What would be the result if a firm's expenses exceed its gross profit? (2)
4 Name four items which could be included in the 'Expenses' figure of £24,500. (4)
5 What is the purpose of the balance sheet? (2)
6 a Give two examples of fixed assets owned by Ritetime. (2)
  b List three current assets. (3)
  c Explain the meaning of 'depreciation'. (2)

7 Give two examples of current liabilities owed by the company. (2)

8 a Calculate the company's working capital. (2)
 b Explain the importance of working capital. (3)

9 a What is a debenture? (1)
 b How much does the company pay each year to its debenture holders? (2)

10 a What is the difference between a bank loan and an overdraft? (2)
 b Why might a business need an overdraft? (2)

11 What will the company's 'reserves' consist of? (2)

12 a Calculate the company's average stock. (2)
 b Calculate the company's rate of turnover. (2)
 c Calculate the company's percentage net profit on turnover. (2)
 d Calculate the company's percentage return on capital. (2)
 e If the current rate of interest paid by your local building society is 10 per cent, would you prefer to invest your money in the company or in the building society? Give reasons for your answer. (4)

Further development

The following ideas could be used to develop this assignment.

1 Consider the ways in which Ritetime could raise capital for expansion.

2 Discuss the ways in which the company could increase its return on capital.

3 Discuss the necessity for proper record-keeping and accounts, including their importance for taxation purposes.

Multiple choice 3

This section contains a series of questions or incomplete sentences followed by four possible responses. In each case select the most appropriate answer.

1 Which of the following would provide a firm with primary data about its markets?
   a Government statistics
   b Questionnaires completed by customers
   c Analysis of customers' complaints
   d Newspaper articles

2 A manufacturer of plumbing supplies is most likely to advertise:
   a on television
   b in trade magazines
   c in local newspapers
   d on local radio.

3 Which of the following is the sales graph likely to be for?
   a Easter eggs
   b Gas fires
   c Fireworks
   d Ice cream

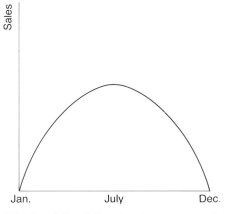

4 Which of the following is an example of 'own label' branding of video tapes?
   a Kodak
   b BASF
   c Panasonic
   d Dixon's

5 Goods deliberately sold at little or no profit to attract trade are called:
   a branded goods
   b kite marks
   c loss leaders
   d impulse purchases.

6 Which of the following advertising media would be most appropriate for a sole trader opening an electrical shop in a small town?
   a Television
   b Local newspaper
   c Trade magazine
   d Sunday magazine

7 Which of the following is used to show a customer the *balance owing for* goods or services supplied?
   a Statement
   b Debit note
   c Quotation
   d Invoice

8 A trader who buys goods for £2,000 and receives 25 per cent trade discount and 5 per cent cash discount will pay:
   a £1,425
   b £1,500
   c £1,575
   d £1,900

9 VAT is levied on:
   a manufacturers only
   b wholesalers only
   c retailers only
   d firms at all stages of the production process.

10 The purpose of an invoice is to:
   a place an order for goods;
   b prove that goods have been delivered;
   c give the cost of goods supplied;
   d state the amount owing at the end of the month.

11 Which of the following is a liability of a business?
   a Company car
   b Bank loan
   c Petty cash
   d Stock of finished goods

12 A firm's variable costs are those which vary directly with:
   a its level of output
   b the Retail Price Index
   c the season of the year
   d its level of profit.

13 During a trading period the rate of stockturn in a business is best defined as the:
   a cost of goods sold
   b average amount of stock at any particular time
   c total sales
   d number of times that average stock is sold.

14 Break-even point in a business is when it makes:
   a the same profit as last year
   b neither a profit nor a loss
   c a small loss but still has money in the bank
   d a profit which compensates for last year's loss.

15 The working capital of a business is:
   a the amount of money it has in the bank;
   b the amount of money owed to it;
   c the difference between its current assets and current liabilities;
   d the total amount of money invested in it.

16 A firm's gross profit is £15,500. What will be the net profit if it has the following expenses? Wages £5,000; Rent £900; Light and Heat £1,250; Depreciation £450; Miscellaneous £1,000.
   a £6,900
   b £8,600
   c £10,000
   d £22,400

17 A retailer buys greetings cards for 18p each and marks them up by 50%. What is the selling price?
   a 24p
   b 27p
   c 30p
   d 36p

In each of the following questions, one or more of the responses is/are correct. Choose the appropriate letter which indicates the correct version.

   a If 1 only is correct.
   b If 3 only is correct.
   c If 1 and 2 only are correct.
   d If 1, 2 and 3 are correct.

18 Which of the following is/are examples of sales promotions?
   1 Free gift offer
   2 'Pop' star opening a record shop
   3 January sales

19 Which of the following is/are advantages of sending goods by road?
   1 Door to door service
   2 Firms can use their own vehicles
   3 Firms can send unlimited loads

20 Which of the following statements about the use of containers in transport is/are true?
   1 They save time and reduce handling costs.
   2 They reduce the risks of loss, theft or damage.
   3 They cannot be used for sending goods abroad.

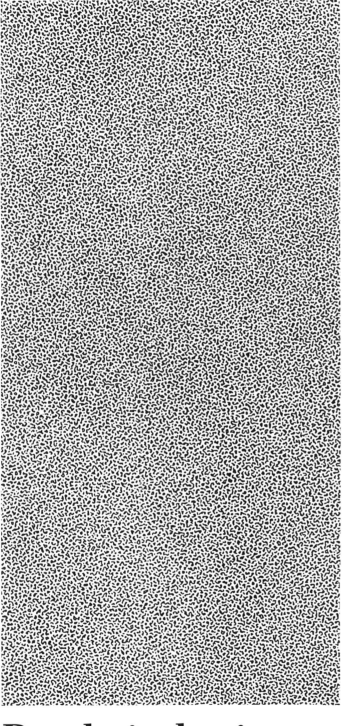

People in business

Assignment 21

Introduction

Assignment 21 is a role play situation which illustrates the importance of job satisfaction. It outlines the problems caused when an employee is offered promotion at work. You will be asked to identify these problems and provide possible solutions.

On completion of this assignment you should be able to:

1 describe the main departments in a large company;
2 identify some factors which affect job promotion;
3 explain the importance of job satisfaction;
4 provide solutions to a personnel problem.

Background information

The management and administration of a business involves the co-ordination of many different functions including finance, marketing, personnel, production, purchasing, transport and customer services. In a large organisation a different department may exist to carry out each of these functions, whilst in a smaller business they may be performed by the owner or just a few people.

Whatever its size, a business's success very often depends upon the quality of the staff it employs. Their efficiency, loyalty, attitudes and enthusiasm can make the difference between a firm making a profit or a loss. Therefore it is important to understand what motivates workers and gives them **job satisfaction**. The more people enjoy their job, the more likely they are to work harder and take a pride in what they do. If workers are unhappy or bored they are less likely to enjoy job satisfaction.

Most people go to work because they need to earn money to pay for food, clothing, housing and social activities. However, there are also many other 'non-money' factors which are important in giving people job satisfaction including:

- good working conditions
- prospects for promotion
- job security
- responsibility to make decisions
- recognition or rewards for work done well
- social factors, for example, friendship of other workers
- status, for example, manager, director, senior clerk.

Choosing a job		
Responsibility and challenge		
Status		
Pay and conditions		
Career prospects		
Location		

Variety and challenge within a professional team

A KEY ROLE

Lead the advances in process technology

Working independently, but not on your own

Join the pacesetters

Variety

Group Marketing Manager

Works Manager

Financial Controller

Superstores Management

Sales Director

Office Manager

Chief Engineer

... Excellent Salaries – Company Car – Good Bonuses

Substantial rewards package + executive car

medical insurance   c £11,000 plus benefits   relocation   Overseas travel

Develop your career through your own success   Training

TRAINEE SALES

AN OUTSTANDING CAREER OPPORTUNITY

promotion check list

Career progression

develop your skills

Location   ★ Based at Burgess Hill, Sussex   Spalding, Lincs   Blackburn,   Sale, Cheshire   Edinburgh   East Anglia

What attracts people to jobs?

73

Career decisions are not always easy

A firm's personnel department is usually responsible for recruiting staff. It also looks after staff welfare, deals with employees' problems at work, keeps staff records, recommends promotions and negotiates with trade unions. It may also be the personnel department which organises a firm's training.

Assignment

You are asked to read and possibly role play the following situation and then complete the tasks that follow.

The people:
HARRY KING, *Purchasing manager*
JACKIE HUNTER, *Clerk/typist*
GRAHAM CARR, *Personnel manager*
PETER BOOTH, *Company solicitor*

Jackie Hunter is 25 and employed as a clerk/typist in the purchasing department of a large chemical company. She is intelligent and cheerful with a pleasant personality. There are a dozen girls in the department and Jackie is a popular and efficient member of the team.

Jackie's job mainly involves ordering goods from suppliers, ensuring that they are received on time and at the price agreed. She has some telephone contact with both the suppliers and with the departments involved within the company. Her typing work is predominantly copy typing although her records show she is a qualified shorthand and audio typist.

Harry King is very pleased with Jackie's work and has said to Graham Carr, on more than one occasion, that she

is worthy of promotion. When Peter Booth needed a new secretary, Graham Carr immediately thought of Jackie. He decided to go and talk to Harry about the position.

GRAHAM CARR: Harry, I have just received a request from Peter Booth for a new secretary. It seems to me that Jackie Hunter would be ideal.
HARRY KING: Maybe, Graham, but she's the best girl I've got. There's no way I want to lose her, promotion or not.
GRAHAM CARR: How much are you paying her?
HARRY KING: £100 per week, but ...
GRAHAM CARR: She'll get a lot more on a secretarial grade, Harry. It's unfair not to give her the chance of a better job with more money.
HARRY KING: . . . I was just thinking, perhaps I could pay her a bit more.
GRAHAM CARR: Maybe, Harry, but you can still only pay her as a typist. She'd get more with Peter.

(The conversation continued for five minutes, after which Harry King finally agreed to let Jackie go on condition that someone good was found to replace her. Later the same day Jackie was called to Graham Carr's office.)

GRAHAM CARR: Good afternoon, Mrs Hunter, please sit down. I've got something to say which I think you'll find very interesting. Do you know Mr Booth, the company's solicitor?
JACKIE HUNTER: Not very well, but I have spoken to him several times.
GRAHAM CARR: Well he needs a new secretary and I've suggested that you would be just the right person. Mr King has agreed to release you, but obviously you need time to consider the job and also to have an interview with Mr Booth.
   Let me tell you a bit about the job. You would be Mr Booth's personal secretary which means running his office by yourself. You would handle all the correspondence and would have to deal with the detailed work involved in preparing customer's contracts. This will probably involve mainly telephone contact, although you will meet some staff and customers who come into the office. The job would mean an immediate increase in salary with a review after six months. How does that interest you?
JACKIE HUNTER: I don't really know. It sounds very responsible and certainly different from my present job. I am not sure if I can do it.
GRAHAM CARR: I am sure with some training that you'd do very well. Why don't you think it over and tell me your decision on Monday?

(By 5.00 pm on Monday, Jackie had not contacted Graham Carr, so he decided to speak to Harry King.)

GRAHAM CARR: Harry, has Jackie said anything to you about Peter's job?
HARRY KING: Afraid not, but I wish she'd make up her mind soon. Since you saw her last week her mind's not been on her work. She's been looking pretty glum and keeps making mistakes. I think the trouble is that she would like the job but doesn't want to leave her friends in the department.

Tasks

1 Draw a simple diagram to show the main departments in a large company. (10)
2 a Briefly describe the main functions of the personnel department using examples from the situation above. (8)
  b Briefly describe the main functions of two other departments. (4)
3 How many girls work in the purchasing department? (1)
4 a Suggest two main reasons why Harry King feels that Jackie is worthy of promotion. (4)
  b Why doesn't he want to lose her? (1)
5 Why does Graham Carr think that Jackie should be given the chance of promotion? (2)
6 In what ways would Jackie's new job be different from what she does now? (5)
7 a Why is Jackie uncertain about whether or not she wants the new job? (4)
  b How is this currently affecting her and the firm? (4)
8 a What does Harry King feel is the main reason why Jackie is uncertain about accepting the new job? (2)
  b How do you think the problem should be resolved? (5)

Further development

The following ideas could be used to develop this assignment.

1 Invite the personnel manager from a local firm to talk about his/her job.
2 Discuss the importance of job satisfaction and determine which factors are most important to the members of your group.
3 Consider what you would have done if you had been in Jackie's situation.

Assignment 22

Introduction

Assignment 22 is a case study of an industrial dispute which can be undertaken as an individual or group exercise. It outlines the workers' demands, the industrial action which they have taken and the effects of these on the company. It then suggests possible ways of solving the problem(s).

On completion of this assignment you should be able to:

1 recognise the nature of industrial disputes and collective bargaining;
2 describe a variety of different forms of industrial action;
3 appreciate the effects of disputes particularly in terms of cost to a firm;
4 demonstrate knowledge of the roles played by different parties in an industrial dispute;
5 appreciate the ways and means of settling industrial disputes.

Background information

The term **industrial relations** is used to cover every aspect of the relationship between a firm's management and its workers. It is important for the successful running of a business that people are happy at work. Good industrial relations therefore help to achieve this and are concerned particularly with employees' conditions of service, working environment and pay.

To represent their interests in industrial relations many workers belong to a **trade union**. A trade union is simply a group of workers who have joined together to bargain with their employers, rather than acting individually. If one man tries to negotiate his own wages he will have very little power, and if he takes **industrial action** it will probably have very little effect on the firm. However, if 1,500 workers join together in a union they are in a much stronger bargaining position.

A national meeting of the NUJ when representatives discuss union policy

The following are some of the main benefits which trade unions seek to achieve for their members:

- better pay
- job security
- shorter working hours
- improved health and safety
- better working conditions
- longer holidays
- better education and training
- worker participation in decision-making.

To achieve these benefits trade unions negotiate with employers by a process known as **collective bargaining**. Each side seeks to get the best deal and to reach a collective agreement which they both find acceptable. However, if trade unions and employers cannot reach an agreement then either side may take industrial action to try and put pressure on the other.

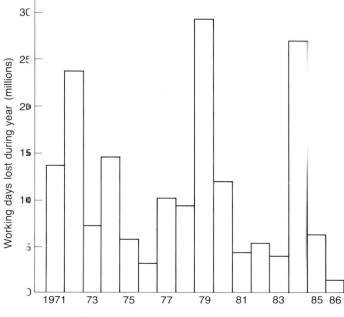

Source: *Employment Gazette.* Department of Employment

UK working days lost through industrial disputes, 1971–1986

Some of the main types of industrial action are as follows:

- **Work to rule** This involves workers following every single rule and regulation in such a way as to slow down work and add to the employer's costs.
- **Go-slow** Workers deliberately work slowly.
- **Overtime ban** Workers may refuse to work more than their normal hours and this may delay orders.
- **Sit-ins** Workers refuse to leave their place of work in protest at some action by their employer. Sit-ins are often used to delay or stop a firm closing down a factory.
- **Strikes** If everything else fails, then workers may decide to strike, i.e. to stop work completely.
- **Lock-out** This is the employer's version of a strike. A firm may literally lock the gates to prevent its employees from coming into work.

Pit ban on overtime to go ahead

THE NATIONAL Union of Mineworkers last night gave the go-ahead for a national overtime ban, to start at midnight on Sunday, accusing British Coal of being "intent on conflict".

The decision followed a day of frantic activity at the conciliation service Acas, involving British Coal, the NUM and the Union of Democratic Mineworkers.

Strike called off

A threatened strike by 150 men in the trim shop at Austin Rover's Longbridge car plant in Birmingham over the sacking of a shop steward for alleged clocking-on irregularities, was called off yesterday. The company is still facing a 24-hour strike threat among its 25,000 hourly-paid workers in a row over pension fund contributions.

Post is hit by wildcat strike

STRIKING postal workers returned to work last night after a lightning wildcat stoppage which left half a million homes and businesses without mail.

They called off their old-fashioned who-does-what dispute 24 hours after insisting that all mail sorted by new recruits should be re-sorted by experienced staff.

TV-am talks

TV-am technicians will meet management tomorrow for the first time since they were locked out eight weeks ago. But both sides appeared yesterday to be willing to concede little.

Air deal offer

Air traffic engineers were last night offered a new pay and conditions package in an effort to stop their overtime ban from becoming an all-out strike.

Firemen vote for a work to rule

MUCH of Britain's fire service was plunged into industrial action, last night.

Firemen in the Midlands, North-West England and Scotland all voted to work to rule in support of 365 men sacked in South Wales.

1,000 laid off in Rover strike

Austin-Rover laid-off 1,000 people at its Longbridge plant in Birmingham, yesterday after 150 car-trimworkers walked out in support of two men dismissed for clocking-on irregularities. One of the sacked men is a shop steward.

Production of the Rover 200 has been halted with an expected loss of about £1 million in output for each day it is at a standstill. Lord Young, Industry Secretary, is due at Longbridge today to see the robotic assembly line.

Industrial action often makes headlines

ACAS

Where unions and employers cannot agree in a dispute they may request the help of the Advisory, Conciliation and Arbitration Service (ACAS). This is an independent body set up by the government to help to improve industrial relations and encourage collective bargaining. ACAS provides four main services:

1 It gives **free advice** to unions and employers.
2 It offers a **conciliation service**. This involves trying to persuade the two sides in a dispute to start talking to each other again.
3 If both sides agree, ACAS can offer **arbitration**. This involves an independent third party listening to the arguments in a dispute and then making a decision which both sides agree to accept.
4 If both sides do not want a binding agreement, then ACAS can arrange **mediation**. This involves a third party listening to the arguments and then suggesting a solution which the two sides can either accept or reject.

Assignment

Read the situation below and complete the tasks that follow.

Manual typewriters have been produced at Bennett's factory, a family owned firm in Castlewood, since it was built in 1950. A large modernisation programme was carried out in the 1970s when the company introduced new technology to enable it to produce electronic typewriters.

Bennett's sells its products throughout the United Kingdom. However, approximately half of its output is exported, mainly to Europe and the Middle East. The company currently employs a total of 50 workers: 34 on the shop floor, 2 in the warehouse, 8 in the office and 6 to drive the company's delivery vans. The factory's normal output is 400 typewriters per week at an ex-works cost of £350 each with a retail mark-up of 50 per cent.

During a recent dispute, the factory was closed for two weeks. The dispute involved the shop floor workers who receive an average weekly wage of £140. They were seeking a wage increase of £7.00 per week plus a reduction from 40 to 38 hours in the working week. They are all members of the GMW which operates a *closed shop* agreement in the plant. The workers claimed that they had maintained production at a high level, the company was making good profits and that their basic working week was longer than most other manufacturing firms in the area.

Bennett's management on the other hand was very concerned about severe competition from the Far East. It felt that a settlement at this level would have to result in higher prices and this would affect sales. Anxious not to lose further production, the company therefore suggested to the union's *shop steward* that a *productivity agreement* might be a sensible way to resolve the dispute. This idea was put to the *branch* membership and rejected.

To settle the dispute quickly, and to avoid further action, the company suggested to the union's officials that the matter be referred to *arbitration*. Both parties agreed, the management insisting that this was subject to an immediate return to work.

Tasks

The following tasks are all based on the case study.

1 a Identify the type of industrial action taken by the workers. (1)
  b Briefly describe three other types of action which they could have taken. (6)
2 a Explain where in the company 'shop floor' employees would expect to work. (1)
  b Calculate the percentage of the total work force employed on the shop floor. (2)
  c Draw a simple diagram to show the breakdown of where people are employed in the company. (2)
3 a Calculate the number of typewriters that were 'lost' during the dispute. (2)
  b Calculate the cost of the dispute to the company in terms of lost production. (2)
  c Calculate the *retail value* of the UK sales 'lost' during the dispute. (2)
4 Find out the name of the trade union to which Bennett's workers belong. (1)
5 Assuming that the workers received their full claim, calculate the weekly wage cost to the company. (2)
6 Assuming that the working week is reduced as demanded, calculate the number of production hours that the company would lose each week. (2)

7 Assuming that a productivity agreement is not reached:
  a how many machines would be produced if the working week is reduced? (2)
  b calculate the weekly cost of the 'lost' production; (2)
  c discuss the effects which it could have on the company. (3)
8 a Explain the basis of the workers' case and the reasons behind the company's attitude to it. (4)
  b Explain why the company was anxious to settle the dispute quickly. (2)
  c Explain the terms *arbitration, branch, closed shop, productivity agreement* and *shop steward*, and the importance of each in resolving the dispute. (10)
  d Draw conclusions and explain what you feel would be a fair outcome to the dispute. (4)

Further development

The following ideas could be used to develop this assignment:

1 Invite a local trade union or ACAS official to talk about his/her work.
2 Invite a personnel officer to talk about industrial relations in his/her firm.
3 Follow a local or national industrial dispute in the news media.

Assignment 23

Payslip

Introduction

Assignment 23 is a study of the factors which determine the 'take home' pay of a person at work and the importance of fringe benefits. It includes a practical exercise to calculate an employee's payslip.

On completion of this assignment you should be able to:

1 explain the difference between gross and net pay;
2 list the most important deductions from wages and salaries;
3 distinguish between statutory (compulsory) and voluntary deductions;
4 calculate an employee's net wage.

Background information

The money which people are paid for work is usually called a wage (if paid weekly) or a salary (if paid monthly). Details of how an employee's pay is calculated is shown on a **payslip** and will include:

Gross pay: how much has been earned. This includes basic pay plus any overtime or bonus payments.

Deductions: how much has been taken out. These can be statutory and/or voluntary.

Net pay or **'take home' pay**: the amount actually received after any deductions.

Statutory deductions, which are compulsory by law, include income tax and National Insurance. The amount employees pay in income tax depends upon their personal circumstances and the rates of tax fixed by the government. Everyone who works is given a Tax Code Number which indicates how much 'free pay' they can earn before paying tax. Income tax is collected under Pay As You Earn (PAYE). Everyone earning over a certain amount also has to pay National Insurance contributions. This money is then used to provide pensions and other state benefits like unemployment and sickness pay.

Voluntary deductions may include payments like superannuation, trade union subscriptions and savings schemes, for example Save As You Earn (SAYE).

In addition to money, many firms offer other incentives to their workers. These are called **fringe benefits**, some examples of which include company cars, luncheon vouchers, pension schemes, staff discounts, medical facilities and transport to work.

Transport

Life assurance

Recreational facilities

Canteen facilities

Help with housing

Saving schemes

Company cars

Fringe benefits

Assignment

The tasks which follow are based on the payroll of Peacock's plc, an engineering company in the West Midlands.

The firm supplies components to the motor industry. It employs 245 shopfloor workers who are paid weekly. There are 78 other staff who are paid monthly by cheque or credit transfer. All employees are paid in arrears.

Tasks

1 a What do the initials plc tell you about Peacocks? (2)
  b How many people does Peacock employ? (1)
  c Where in the company will the shopfloor employees work? (1)
  d Explain the statement 'all employees are paid in arrears'. (2)
  e Briefly explain what happens to the salary of an employee who is paid by credit transfer. (2)
2 Malcolm Jenkins, who is 16, has worked as a trainee storekeeper for the firm for three months. He is paid at a basic rate of £60 for a 40 hour week. Last week he worked four hours overtime for which he is paid at time-and-a-half.
  a How much is Malcolm paid per hour? (2)
  b How much did he earn in overtime last week? (2)
  c What was his gross pay for the week? (2)
3 To calculate Malcolm's 'take home pay' it is necessary to have details of any statutory and voluntary deductions.
  The following information relates to last week.
  PAYE due is £7.50 on the basic wage plus 25 per cent of any overtime pay.
  National Insurance due is at 5 per cent of earnings over £41 per week.

Sports and Social Club deductions are 50p per week.
Trade Union subscriptions are 75p per week.
SAYE deductions are £2.50 per week.
  a Explain the difference between statutory and voluntary deductions. (4)
  b Give two examples of each which would appear on Malcolm's payslip. (2)
  c How much did Malcolm pay in tax? Show how you worked this out. (2)
  d How much did he pay in National Insurance? Show how you worked this out. (2)
  e Name two of the main benefits provided by the National Insurance scheme. (2)
  f What is a Trade Union? Explain why you think Malcolm decided to join a union. (5)
4 a Using the information in Tasks 2 and 3, copy and complete Malcolm's payslip below. (4)
  b Explain what is meant by the figures in each of these columns in the payslip below:
    ● Works No.
    ● Tax Code
    ● Taxable pay to date
    ● Tax to date. (4)
  c Calculate the total deductions and Malcolm's net pay for the week. (4)
5 Peacock's offer its workers a number of fringe benefits.
  a What are fringe benefits? (2)
  b Suggest some fringe benefits which Malcolm might enjoy. (5)

Further development

The following ideas could be used to develop this assignment.

1 Would *you* prefer to be paid a wage in cash or be paid directly into your bank account? Give your reasons.
2 If you were offered a low wage with good fringe benefits, or a high wage but with very few fringe benefits, consider which you would choose and why.
3 Imagine Malcolm has been moved to another section of the firm. Prepare a job advertisement to attract someone to replace him.

NAME	WORKS NO	DATE	TAX CODE	GROSS WAGE	OVERTIME/ ADDITIONAL PAY		TOTAL GROSS PAY
M JENKINS	4793/3		270L				
TAXABLE PAY TO DATE	TAX TO DATE		TAX THIS PAYMENT	NI	UNION	SAVE	SPORTS & SOCIAL
£760.00	£98.00						
	TOTAL DEDUCTIONS				NET PAY		

F

Assignment 24

Getting the message

Introduction

Assignment 24 is a series of exercises to develop an understanding of the main methods of communication used in a business. It can be carried out as an individual or group activity.

On completion of this assignment you should be able to:

1 explain the need for effective communication in business;
2 describe the main internal and external methods of communication;
3 describe written, spoken and visual methods of communication;
4 appreciate the impact of new technology on methods of communication.

Background information

Communication is essential in any business and to be effective it must be quick, accurate and readily understood. Communication is a two-way process to enable information to be passed from one person or organisation to another. It must involve four elements:

1 The **sender** or source of the communication.
2 The **message** or content of what is being communicated.
3 The **medium** or means by which which the communication travels, for example letter, telephone.
4 The **audience** or people to whom the communication is being sent.

Communication may be verbal or non-verbal, formal or informal, internal or external and all forms are important to a business.

'Verbal communication!'

Carphones are an important new development in communications technology

In the UK, the major suppliers of external communication services are the Post Office and British Telecom. These organisations provide a wide range of national and international communication systems, which are becoming increasingly sophisticated with the introduction of new technology.

It is also important for good communication that information can be stored or filed so that it can be quickly located and retrieved when required. However, there is no one correct method of filing or storage and consequently each firm must set up a system most suited to its own needs.

Nowadays more and more organisations are making increased use of computerised filing systems for communicating and storing information and data.

Assignment

Read the situation described below and then complete the tasks that follow.

You work in the administrative department of Andrews, an expanding public company which manufactures a range of tinned foods. Your training officer, Mr Thorpe, is concerned that several new employees seem to have very little knowledge or understanding of office work and communications. He decides to ask you to prepare brief notes for them.

Tasks

1 Outline the basic functions of an office and briefly describe the work involved. (5)
2 The following terms are all used in the background information. Define each one using examples where appropriate:
   a Verbal communication
   b Non-verbal communication
   c Informal communication
   d Formal communication
   e Internal communication
   f External communication
   g New technology
   h International communication systems
   i Public company
   j Computerised filing system
   (10)
3 Identify the external methods of communication in the following list:
   a Local newspaper advertisement
   b Market Research Survey
   c Closed circuit television
   d Social club notice
   e Manager's meeting
   f Sales literature
   g Credit note
   h Price list
   i House journal
   (2½)
4 List five main methods of communication provided by the Post Office and British Telecom which Andrews may use. (2½)
5 Now list and briefly describe five other methods of communication which are likely to be used by Andrews. State whether they would be used for internal or external communication. (5)

6 Match the correct term from the box with the appropriate business use from the list beneath it.

1 Freepost	5 Memorandum	9 Statement
2 Facsimile	6 Press release	10 Confravision
3 Invoice	7 Word processing	
4 Microfilm	8 Prestel	

   a When space is a problem for filing
   b To enable a firm to transmit an exact copy of a document
   c When an internal means of communication is needed
   d A sales conference where a firm's four branches are linked together
   e To encourage replies to advertisements   (5)

7 During the course of the day you are asked to carry out the duties a–e below. From the following box, select the appropriate method of communication which you would use in each case. Use each method *once* only and give a reason(s) for your choice:

Memorandum	Confravision	Telephone
Air Mail	Telex	Intelpost
Radio-phone	International	Letter Post
Parcel Post	Telegram	

   a Ask a supplier in Manchester about a delivery of goods which is urgently required.
   b Send a catalogue to a potential customer in Paris.
   c Send an urgent message to a Canadian supplier.
   d Transmit a legal document to the Glasgow branch office.
   e Ask the computer systems manager, who is out of the office for the day, to confirm the holiday arrangements for his section.   (5)

8 a Explain why Andrews needs to communicate with each of the following and the main methods it is likely to use:
   ● employees
   ● suppliers
   ● customers
   ● local authority
   ● government.   (10)
   b Since Andrews is a public limited company, describe one other group of people it would need to communicate with and explain how it would do this, giving reasons for your answer.   (15)

Further development

The following ideas could be used to develop this assignment.

1 Examine the impact of new technology, particularly the growth of VDUs and electronic mail, on external and internal communications and the storage of information.
2 Consider the factors which should be taken into account when deciding whether or not to retain data for filing.
3 Discuss the importance of effective communication and how it can affect the motivation of staff in an organisation.

Multiple choice 4

This section contains a series of questions or incomplete sentences followed by four possible responses. In each case select the most appropriate answer.

1 In an industrial dispute workers may take all but which *one* of the following forms of action?
   a Strike
   b Overtime ban
   c Work to rule
   d Lock-out

2 A shop steward's role includes all but which *one* of the following?
   a Recruiting new members
   b Negotiating with management
   c Organising social activities
   d Dealing with problems on 'the spot'

3 The NUT is an example of:
   a a craft union
   b a general union
   c an industrial union
   d a white collar union.

4 When an employee leaves a job he/she is given a:
   a P11
   b P45
   c P60
   d bonus.

5 The following are functions of a trade union except:
   a to increase sex discrimination
   b to improve working conditions
   c to protect its members' jobs
   d to negotiate for better pay.

6 Which of the following items is a statutory deduction from an employee's wage?
   a Income tax
   b Trade union subscription
   c Superannuation
   d Company savings scheme

7 Mary Brennan is paid a basic wage of £2 per hour for a 35 hour week. Last week she worked 5 hours overtime for which she is paid at time-and-a-half. How much much did she earn for the week?
   a £40
   b £70
   c £80
   d £85

8 A curriculum vitae is:
   a a reference
   b an invitation to an interview
   c a summary of a person's career and qualifications
   d a job description.

9 All but which *one* of the following would be considered as the 'fringe benefits' of a job?
 a Free travel to and from work
 b Subsidised canteen meals
 c Payment by bank credit transfer
 d Discounts on the firm's products

10 By law, a Contract of Employment must include details of all but which *one* of the following?
 a Job title
 b Promotion prospects
 c Hours of work and holidays
 d Rate of pay

11 Which of the following would be used to find the names and telephone numbers of local newsagents?
 a Yellow Pages
 b Post Office Guide
 c The Phone Book
 d Local street map

12 Which of the following is a formal method of communication?
 a Staff notice board
 b Social event
 c Lunchtime discussion
 d Recruitment interview

13 This diagram is an example of:
 a a line graph
 b a bar chart
 c a pie chart
 d a pictograph.

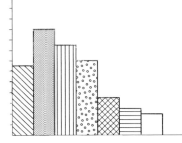

14 Which of the following is a form of visual communication?
 a 'Grapevine'
 b Telephone
 c Memorandum
 d Intercom

15 The minutes of a meeting are:
 a a record of the matters discussed
 b the rules saying how it should be organised
 c a list of issues to be discussed
 d a report from another committee.

16 Proof of delivery is provided by all except which *one* of the following postal services?
 a Recorded Delivery
 b Certificate of Posting
 c Cash on Delivery
 d Registered Post

17 Which *one* of the following telecommunication services does *not* provide two-way communication?
 a Ceefax
 b Prestel
 c Datel
 d Confravision

In each of the following questions, one or more of the responses is/are correct. Choose the appropriate letter which indicates the correct version.
 a If 1 only is correct.
 b If 3 only is correct.
 c If 1 and 2 only are correct.
 d if 1, 2 and 3 are correct.

18 Which of the following statements is/are correct?
 1 Income tax is collected under PAYE
 2 Gross pay is the amount earned before any deductions
 3 'Flexitime' is another term for shiftwork

19 Computers and word processors can be used in a business for:
 1 the storage and retrieval of information
 2 preparing the payroll
 3 automatic updating of stock records.

20 Which of the following is/are external methods of communication?
 1 Compliment slips
 2 Local advertising
 3 Letters to customers

Government influence on business activity

Assignment 25

Introduction

Assignment 25 is a case study based on a proposal by British Coal to develop a new 'superpit' at Southawk. It considers the social costs and benefits to the local community if the proposal goes ahead and the role of pressure groups in trying to prevent it. It is recommended that you undertake this assignment in small groups.

On completion of this assignment you should be able to:

1 explain how the location of a business may be affected by social as well as commercial factors;
2 appreciate that businesses are motivated by profit;
3 recognise the part played in business by government legislation and local authorities;
4 explain the roles of pressure groups in society.

Background information

Cost-benefit analysis

When the government is considering a major item of public expenditure, for example, developing a new motorway or coal mine, it may decide to carry out a cost-benefit analysis. Such studies attempt to evaluate all the costs and benefits which are expected to affect the community. These costs can be both private and social.

The **private cost** of something is essentially the price which an individual or organisation pays for it, for example, buying a car for £5,000. The **private benefits** of this purchase are difficult to estimate but will include the convenience, flexibility and saving from not using other forms of transport.

However, there will also be wider social costs and social benefits from this decision. **Social costs** are those which affect the community and will include the extra traffic congestion, noise, loss of business to public or other transport, pollution from exhaust fumes and the increased wear and tear of the roads. The **social benefits** which will result include a more flexible, mobile work force and additional employment in garages—for petrol, parts and servicing, and in road maintenance. There will also be more government revenue from the tax on petrol sales. All economic activities will result in a similar mixture of costs and benefits.

Social costs and benefits of mining

Assignment

Read the situation below and complete the tasks that follow.

In recent years British Coal has embarked on a course of modernisation involving the development of 'superpits' using the latest technology. It is currently seeking planning permission from the Local Authority for the development of a site which is in a green belt location at Southawk. However, it is encountering considerable local opposition to its proposals.

It is anticipated that it will take some ten or eleven years for the pit to develop to full production, and that it will then have a working life of approximately 35 years. Whilst the pit is in full production considerable quantities of coal, earth and rubble will be brought to the surface. Waste from the mine will be tipped into nearby quarries to reclaim valuable farming land. The coal will be moved by road and rail transport which will involve some ten trains

and approximately 700 lorry-loads per day.

To facilitate these movements, a new road will be constructed from the pit head to an existing trunk road, and a new railway line, complete with sidings, will be built to link the mine with the existing rail network. British Coal's recent investigations have shown that the coal at Southawk is of very high quality. It is also comparatively easy to mine because it is available in a thick seam near the surface.

The coal will mainly be used for fuelling power stations to produce electricity. Although this type of coal is available in other areas it will become increasingly scarce towards the end of the century. The development of this project is expected to have a significant effect on local employment, both for those directly involved in the mining industry and for those who provide ancillary services. Recent estimates suggest that 1500–1800 new jobs may be created.

However, the local council and local residents are acutely aware that there could be considerable environmental damage from this plan. Groups opposed to the superpit development claim that great damage will be caused to the environment and this will far outweigh any commercial advantage.

British Coal acknowledges many of these problems and, indeed, has paid many millions of pounds in compensation to property owners throughout the country as a result of damage caused by the subsidence from other mining operations. Even so, British Coal feels that this development at Southawk is vital for the future profitability of the industry and that it must proceed as quickly as possible.

A modern coal mine

SOUTHAWK

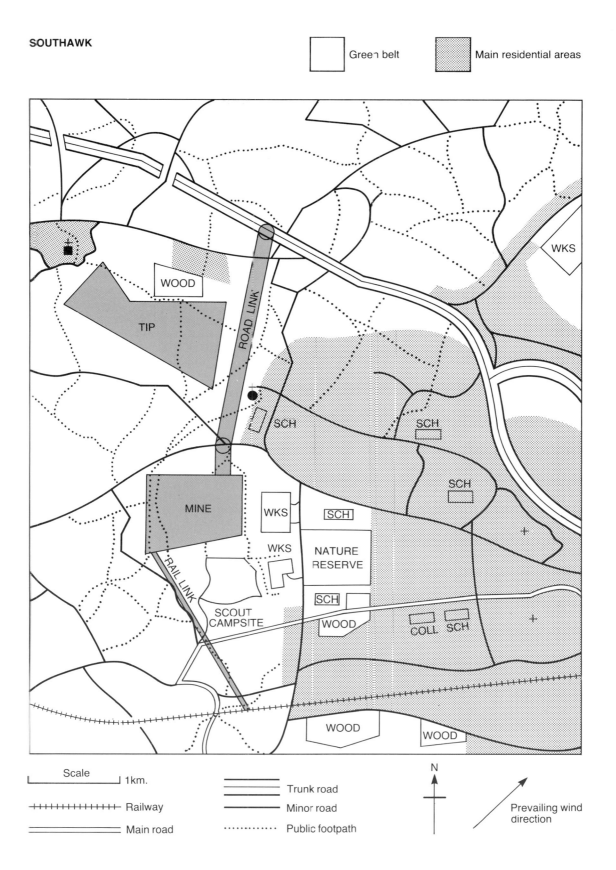

Scale |_____| 1km.

++++++++++++++ Railway

═══════════ Main road

═══════════ Trunk road

─────────── Minor road

·········· Public footpath

N

Prevailing wind direction

Southawk proposed development

Tasks

Complete the following tasks in your own words.

1 Explain what is meant by a 'green belt' and give an example of one in your area. (4)

2 Explain the main arguments *for* and *against* the superpit development at Southawk. (16)

3 Describe the sort of action which you could take if you wished to stop the pit. Which local and national organisations could you call upon for support? (5)

4 How could you rally support for British Coal's proposals? What sort of action could you take to convince people that the development of the pit would be good for the area? (5)

5 Give your evaluation of whether or not the development should go ahead. Present your views in a short essay of about 300 words. (20)

Further development

The following ideas could be used to develop this assignment.

1 If there is a local industrial, commercial or shopping development taking place, prepare arguments both for and against it and draw your own conclusions on its desirability.

2 This could be expanded into group work involving a site visit, the collection of relevant data (newspaper articles etc) and a formal presentation of your findings using visual aids.

3 Consider the social costs and benefits that would result if a new road was built which bypassed the area where you live.

Assignment 26

Introduction

Assignment 26 is an investigation into the likely effects of a change in the present Sunday trading laws. Market research has shown that most people would like the present law changed so that it becomes easier to understand. You are asked to examine the arguments for and against all shops being allowed to open for seven days a week and then prepare a short essay giving your own opinions. For this assignment you will need to work in small groups.

On completion of this assignment you should be able to:

1 explain the issues involved in Sunday trading;
2 be aware of the main government legislation in respect of retailing;
3 summarise the main arguments for and against Sunday trading;
4 appreciate the role of pressure groups in society.

Background information

Most high streets are silent and empty on Sundays

Sunday trading

As you will know, at the moment most shops are closed on Sundays whilst some also close for a day or half day during the week. The main reason for this is that shopping hours are controlled by law, the most important of which is the Shops Act 1950. This states:

- that shops must be closed by 9.00 pm on a late day and 8.00 pm on any other day, and

- that only certain goods can be sold on Sundays.

However, this Act only applies to England and Wales. Only hairdressers cannot open on Sundays in Scotland, whilst Northern Ireland has its own Shops Act. In some areas, the local authority which enforces the shopping laws will prosecute certain retailers who trade on Sundays. However, in other areas they 'turn a blind eye' and take no action. This is because, by law, unless the local authority gives special permission, only certain goods can be sold on Sundays. Some retailers also open very late during the week and again this is often against the law.

Tradition dies as shoppers take to the crowded High Streets

Sunday trading plans backed

Sunday traders' stocking hitch

FIGHT OVER SUNDAY BAN ON TRADING

Sunday traders 'left alone unless people complain'

Vicar hits at Sunday trading

Sabbath pubs move resisted

Sunday trading dispute

If shops are allowed to stay open for seven days it will affect a lot of people in different ways, for example, **consumers** like you and your friends will be able to go to the shops whenever you like. However, if you are an **employee** it may mean that you must work on a Sunday. **Religious bodies** like the Church may feel that it will prevent people from going to church, whilst the **government** might argue that it will create more jobs. **Employers**, on the other hand, might be concerned about the extra costs which it would involve. Sunday trading would also affect many other groups of workers, for example, the **police force**, and those working in **banks** and in **public transport**.

Assignment

Read the situation below and complete the tasks that follow.

During the past 30 years the government has set up a number of committees to review the laws relating to Sunday trading. However, so far any attempts to change the present laws have been unsuccessful. Mr Humphrey Froggart, MP, is determined to see a new Bill introduced in the next session of Parliament. He argues that:

We have a very confused situation at present where it is lmost impossible to enforce a wide range of contradictory legislation. It is hard to understand why we are allowed to buy some things on a Sunday but not others; for example, you can buy a teenage magazine but not a Bible; a Chinese takeaway but not fish and chips. These anomalies need to be clarified in the public interest as soon as possible.

Just another day . . .
This picture illustrates some of the likely effects if all shops were to open on Sundays and may help you with Task 5.

Tasks

Carefully re-read the background information and situation above and then, working in small groups, carry out Tasks 1–6.

1 Name the major law which controls the hours when shops are allowed to open.
2 List at least five different *types* of retailers in your area which you know open on a Sunday, for example, newsagents.
3 Within your group make a note of any of the following items which you know to have been bought on a Sunday:

a Fresh fruit and vegetables
b Fresh flowers
c Confectionery
d Tobacco
e Cigarettes
f Medicines
g Newspapers
h Restaurant meals and refreshments
i Motor accessories
j Ice cream

k Antiques
l Furniture
m Electrical goods
n Cars
o Fish and chips
p Books
q Greetings cards
r Clothing

s Hardware goods
t Garden equipment

4 The list in Task 3 will help you to realise the confused state of the present Sunday trading laws. It is difficult to understand why it is legal for items a–j to be sold on a

Sunday but against the law to sell items k–t. Can your group suggest possible reasons why it is illegal for items k–t to be sold on a Sunday?

5 Sunday trading would affect a lot of people in different ways. Your group will be asked by your teacher to represent one of the following:

the government,
employers,
consumers,
employees or
religious bodies.

Your task is to prepare, for the group which you represent, a list of what you feel are the main arguments *for* and/or *against* Sunday trading. It may be useful to contact some of the following:

Consumers Association	Local authority
USDAW	Local councillors
Employers associations	Local MP
The National Chamber of Trade	Local Chamber of Trade/Commerce
Lord's Day Observance Society	Local churches
Retail Consortium	Local consumer groups

National and local newspaper magazine articles may also provide useful information.

6 Each group should now make a short presentation of their findings in Tasks 1–5 to the rest of the class. You may decide to elect just one spokesperson or ask each member of the group to say something.

7 Finally, *on your own*, write a short essay (approximately 350 words) entitled 'Sunday Trading'. In it you should outline the present situation and say whether or not you are in favour of a change in the Sunday trading laws. State to what extent you think that they should be altered, if at all, giving your reasons.　　(50)

Further development

The following ideas could be used to develop this assignment.

1 Other groups could be formed to represent the interests of those indirectly affected by Sunday trading, for example, the police, banks, providers of public transport, and local communities.
2 A vote could be held to discover the class' views on Sunday trading. This could take place both *before* and *after* the various tasks have been completed and the results compared and discussed.
3 You could try to discover when Sunday trading was last debated in Parliament and the result. This could be done by contacting your local MP, and at the same time you could ask for his/her views on the issue.
4 A guest speaker could be invited from one or more of the interested pressure groups.

Assignment 27

Where are the jobs?

Introduction

Assignment 27 uses regional unemployment statistics, a map of the assisted areas and a news article to illustrate the problems of unemployment and the effect of the government's policies with regard to job creation. This assignment can be undertaken individually or in groups.

On completion of this assignment you should be able to:

1 understand the main causes of unemployment;
2 explain the 'regional problem';
3 name some government measures to alleviate unemployment;
4 comment on current unemployment trends.

A demonstration against high unemployment

Background information

When industries cannot sell all the goods which they make, factories have to close down and people lose their jobs. The demand for services also falls because people do not have money to spend on them. Very soon, rising unemployment can lead to a severe economic slump or depression.

This is what happened in the 1930s when unemployment was high throughout the UK, although some areas suffered much more badly than others. Since then, successive governments have introduced special measures to try to solve regional unemployment and the social and economic problems which it brings.

Since the Second World War, changes in demand, foreign competition and the introduction of new technology have all led to a decline in some of the UK's main industries like coal, shipbuilding and textiles. This has resulted in high unemployment in the areas where these industries are located.

At the same time, some areas of the UK have become very prosperous, attracting many people to move there. However, this has brought with it the problems of overcrowding, such as traffic congestion, pollution, housing shortages and overstretched education, medical and social services.

It is this problem of **regional imbalance** which government policies try to solve. They aim to attract industries away from the congested areas and into the areas of high and persistent unemployment. To do this the government prevents industrial development in certain areas and offers help to the areas with the most serious unemployment problems. Some of the measures used include:

- **grants** or **cheap loans**: for buildings and equipment
- **special tax allowances**
- **provision of ready-built factories**
- **development of new towns**, like Skelmersdale and Peterlee.

Whenever possible, the government has itself set an example by moving its own departments into assisted areas, thus the Training Commission is located in Sheffield, Girobank in Bootle and the Department of Health and Social Security in Newcastle.

Assignment

Having read the background information, study the statistics, map and news article below. Then complete the tasks that follow.

Region	Percentage of all employees			
	Jan '73	Nov '78	Jan '87	Oct '87
South East	2.0	3.9	8.5	6.8
East Anglia	2.6	4.7	9.3	6.7
South West	3.4	6.4	10.4	8.0
West Midlands	3.0	5.4	13.8	11.1
East Midlands	2.8	4.8	11.4	8.9
Yorks and Humberside	3.8	5.8	13.8	11.4
North West	4.6	7.2	14.3	12.6
North	6.0	8.6	16.9	14.0
Wales	4.9	8.3	14.3	12.3
Scotland	6.1	7.8	15.1	13.2
Northern Ireland	7.5	10.9	19.3	18.2
Average	4.1	6.7	13.4	11.2

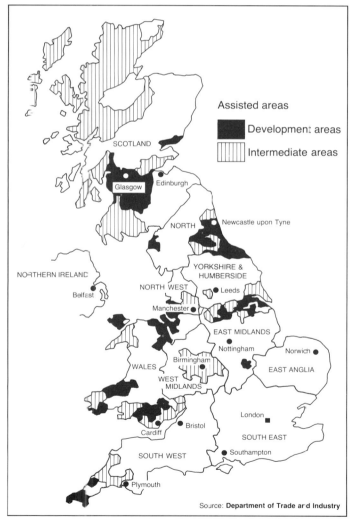

Source: **Department of Trade and Industry**

How unemployment affects the regions

UNEMPLOYMENT DROPS TO LOWEST LEVEL FOR FIVE YEARS

UNEMPLOYMENT in October 1987 fell to its lowest level since July, 1982, the 16th successive fall. Over the past six months the total has fallen by a record 50,500 a month compared to 23,600 a month in the previous half-year to April.

Record fall

Total unemployment showed its largest 12-month fall on record, dropping 485,770 since October 1986 to 2,751,384. It includes a record fall of 119,631 in unemployed adults to 2,668,158, the lowest level at this time of year since October 1981 (2,592,200).

The number of unemployed school-leavers at 83,226 was at its best October level since 1979 (56,500). Kenneth Fowler announcing the figures said: "Unemployment has fallen in all parts of the country and internationally our performance has been better than many of our major competitors. Over the past 12 months, the rate of unemployment has dropped by over 1.5 percentage points. In many European countries, like Germany, France and Italy, the unemployment rate has increased".

Mr Fowler added that the United Kingdom employment position was strong and the latest figures on young unemployed were "most encouraging". But the Government's priority now had to be to consider new training measures to assist the long-term jobless.

Special Government measures were assisting 378,800 people in September, 9,550 more than September, 1986. They included 229,000 on Community Programmes; 96,000 on Enterprise Allowance Schemes; 24,000 on Job Training Schemes; and 428,000 on the two-year Youth Training Scheme. Vacancies at job centres in October totalled 261,400, a 14,800 rise on September and a 25 per cent increase over October last year. Community Programme vacancies increased to 32,000, which is 2,900 below October 19, 1986. Pointing out that the number of unfilled vacancies was at yet another record level, Mr Fowler added that 372,000 extra jobs had been created in the year — 206,000 full-time and 166,000 part-time. The total employed labour force now stands at 24,359,000.

Tasks

1 Briefly explain three possible reasons why unemployment might rise. (3)
2 Explain what is meant by 'regional imbalance' and list some of the problems which it can cause. (5)
3 What are 'assisted areas', who assists them and how are they assisted? (2)
4 a Which four regions have the highest unemployment? (2)
  b Which four regions have the lowest unemployment? (2)
5 What general trends can be identified from the statistics on regional unemployment? Use examples to illustrate your answer. (4)
6 From the map identify:
  a two towns or cities which are in 'development areas'; (2)
  b two which are in 'intermediate areas'. (2)
7 Name three towns or cities which are *not* in assisted areas. Explain why you think this is so. (5)
8 In October 1987 how many people were:
  a unemployed, (1)
  b employed? (1)
9 Calculate the comparative figures for October 1986. How many people were:
  a unemployed, (2)
  b employed? (2)
10 a How many people are being helped by special government measures? (1)
  b Give four examples of such measures. (2)
  c What will the government's future priority be regarding unemployment? (2)
11 What are 'unfilled vacancies' and why are they important? (2)
12 What evidence is there to support Mr Fowler's view that the UK's employment position is strong? (10)

Further development

The following ideas could be used to develop this assignment.

1 Find out further details about some of the government measures to help the unemployed.
2 Visit your local Job Centre and find out about the work which it does.
3 If your town is in an assisted area (if not contact one that is), find out what help is available for businesses located there. Look for advertisements in national newspapers or write to the Department of Trade and Industry for information.

Assignment 28

The Budget

Introduction

Assignment 28 is about the main sources of government income from taxation and its expenditure on goods and services for the community. It involves the analysis of data about the Budget.

On completion of this assignment you should be able to:

1 understand the role of the Budget in regulating the economy;
2 explain the main forms of taxation;
3 describe the effects of changes in taxation;
4 appreciate the significance to firms and individuals of government financial measures.

Background information

The Budget

In March or April each year, the Chancellor of the Exchequer presents a Budget to Parliament. This is a financial statement which gives the government's estimated revenue and expenditure for the last financial year, and forecasts for the next year. It also gives details of any proposed tax changes. Sometimes 'mini' Budgets are announced at other times of the year.

The Budget has two main functions. It enables the government to:

- **Regulate the economy** by controlling the demand for goods and services.
- **Redistribute income and wealth** among the various sections of the community.

Taxes are classified as direct or indirect. **Direct taxes** are levied directly on the income or wealth of individuals and companies, for example income tax and corporation tax. **Indirect taxes** are levied on the expenditure on goods and services and are therefore paid indirectly to the tax authorities, for example, Value Added Tax (VAT) and Customs and Excise Duties. The government uses the money which it collects in taxation to help provide goods and services for the nation. Some of these are provided centrally, for example, unemployment and other benefits, defence and the National Health Service. Others like education, police and fire services are provided by the local authority using money collected from rates and government grants. The government also frequently pays for some of its expenditure by borrowing.

Assignment

The following tasks are based on the background information provided and the article 'Putting the Budget together'.

Tasks

1 a What do you understand by 'The Budget'? (2)
  b In which month is it usually presented to Parliament? (1)
  c Explain the two main purposes of the Budget. (4)
2 Draw two pie diagrams, one to illustrate the main categories of government income and the other to illustrate the main items of expenditure. (6)
3 Describe and give two examples of each of the following terms:
  a direct taxes
  b indirect taxes
  c cash benefits
  d benefits in kind. (12)
4 Read the section entitled 'The Treasury's Balancing Act' and complete the following:
  a explain what is meant by the 'balancing act'; (3)
  b outline two courses of action which the government can take if it is unable to balance the Budget. (2)
5 Read the section, 'The main spending departments', and name two organisations which may try to influence the government in deciding its Budget measures. Explain why they may wish to do this. (4)
6 Changes in taxation can affect people and businesses in many ways. For example, if the duty on wines and spirits is increased, it is likely that people will buy less alcohol. This could lead to falling sales and profits for businesses. In turn, they may employ less staff leading to an increase in unemployment.

Study the possible changes in taxation in List A. Now match them against the most likely effects from List B. Each effect in List B should be used once only.

> List A: **Taxation changes**
> 1 Increase in rate of VAT
> 2 Reduction in rate of VAT
> 3 Increase in petrol duty
> 4 Increase in income tax
> 5 Reduction in income tax

7 a Calculate the percentage of direct taxation which is accounted for by income tax. (2)
  b Suggest two main advantages and two main disadvantages of income tax as a means of raising revenue. (4)

Putting the Budget together

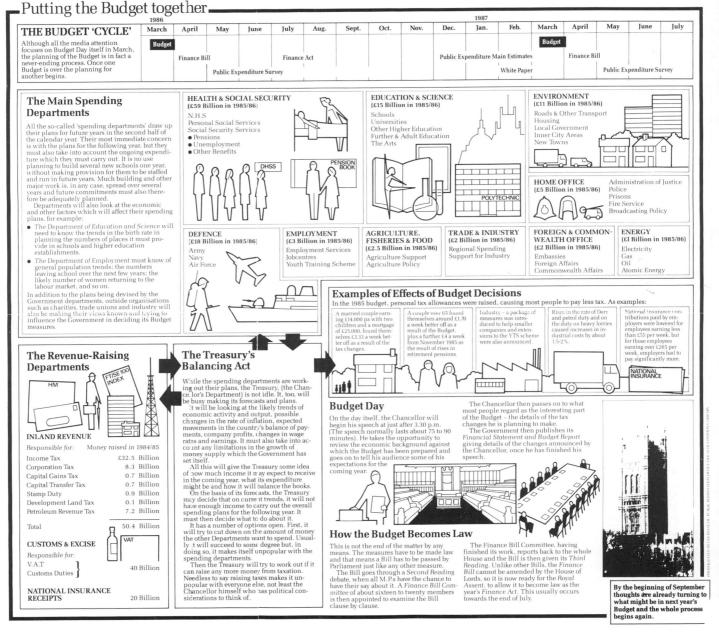

THE BUDGET 'CYCLE'

Although all the media attention focuses on Budget Day itself in March, the planning of the Budget is in fact a never-ending process. Once one Budget is over the planning for another begins.

1986										1987						
March	April	May	June	July	Aug.	Sept.	Oct.	Nov.	Dec.	Jan.	Feb.	March	April	May	June	July
Budget												Budget				
	Finance Bill			Finance Act						Public Expenditure Main Estimates			Finance Bill			
		Public Expenditure Survey									White Paper			Public Expenditure Survey		

The Main Spending Departments

All the so-called 'spending departments' draw up their plans for future years in the second half of the calendar year. Their most immediate concern is with the plans for the following year, but they must also take into account the ongoing expenditure which they must carry out. It is no use planning to build several new schools one year, without making provision for them to be staffed and run in future years. Much building and other major work is, in any case, spread over several years and future commitments must also therefore be adequately planned.

Departments will also look at the economic and other factors which will affect their spending plans, for example:

● *The Department of Education and Science* will need to know the trends in the birth rate in planning the numbers of places it must provide in schools and higher education establishments.

● *The Department of Employment* must know of general population trends; the numbers leaving school over the next few years; the likely number of women returning to the labour market, and so on.

In addition to the plans being devised by the Government departments, outside organisations such as charities, trade unions and industry will also be making their views known and trying to influence the Government in deciding its Budget measures.

HEALTH & SOCIAL SECURITY
(£59 Billion in 1985/86)
N.H.S
Personal Social Services
Social Security Services
● Pensions
● Unemployment
● Other Benefits

EDUCATION & SCIENCE
(£15 Billion in 1985/86)
Schools
Universities
Other Higher Education
Further & Adult Education
The Arts

ENVIRONMENT
(£11 Billion in 1985/86)
Roads & Other Transport
Housing
Local Government
Inner City Areas
New Towns

HOME OFFICE
(£5 Billion in 1985/86)
Administration of Justice
Police
Prisons
Fire Service
Broadcasting Policy

DEFENCE
(£18 Billion in 1985/86)
Army
Navy
Air Force

EMPLOYMENT
(£3 Billion in 1985/86)
Employment Services
Jobcentres
Youth Training Scheme

AGRICULTURE, FISHERIES & FOOD
(£2.5 Billion in 1985/86)
Agriculture Support
Agriculture Policy

TRADE & INDUSTRY
(£2 Billion in 1985/86)
Regional Spending
Support for Industry

FOREIGN & COMMON-WEALTH OFFICE
(£2 Billion in 1985/86)
Embassies
Foreign Affairs
Commonwealth Affairs

ENERGY
(£1 Billion in 1985/86)
Electricity
Gas
Oil
Atomic Energy

Examples of Effects of Budget Decisions

In the 1985 budget, personal tax allowances were raised, causing most people to pay less tax. As examples:

A married couple earning £14,000 pa with two children and a mortgage of £25,000, found themselves £3.33 a week better off as a result of the tax changes.

A couple over 65 found themselves around £1.70 a week better off as a result of the Budget, plus a further £4 a week from November 1985 as the result of rises in retirement pensions.

Industry – a package of measures was introduced to help smaller companies and extensions to the YTS scheme were also announced.

Rises in the rate of Derv and petrol duty and on the duty on heavy lorries caused increases in industrial costs by about 1.5-2%.

National insurance contributions paid by employers were lowered for employees earning less than £55 per week, but for those employees earning over £265 per week, employers had to pay significantly more.

The Revenue-Raising Departments

INLAND REVENUE
Responsible for: Money raised in 1984/85

Income Tax	£32.5	Billion
Corporation Tax	8.3	Billion
Capital Gains Tax	0.7	Billion
Capital Transfer Tax	0.7	Billion
Stamp Duty	0.9	Billion
Development Land Tax	0.1	Billion
Petroleum Revenue Tax	7.2	Billion
Total	50.4	Billion

CUSTOMS & EXCISE
Responsible for:
V.A.T
Customs Duties } 40 Billion

NATIONAL INSURANCE RECEIPTS 20 Billion

The Treasury's Balancing Act

While the spending departments are working out their plans, the Treasury, (the Chancellor's Department) is not idle. It, too, will be busy making its forecasts and plans.

It will be looking at the likely trends of economic activity and output, possible changes in the rate of inflation, expected movements in the country's balance of payments, company profits, changes in wage rates and earnings. It must also take into account any limitations in the growth of money supply which the Government has set itself.

All this will give the Treasury some idea of how much income it may expect to receive in the coming year, what its expenditure might be and how it will balance the books.

On the basis of its forecasts, the Treasury may decide that on current trends, it will not have enough income to carry out the overall spending plans for the following year. It must then decide what to do about it.

It has a number of options open. First, it will try to cut down on the amount of money the other Departments want to spend. Usually, it will succeed to some degree but, in doing so, it makes itself unpopular with the spending departments.

Then the Treasury will try to work out if it can raise any more money from taxation. Needless to say raising taxes makes it unpopular with everyone else, not least the Chancellor himself who has political considerations to think of.

Budget Day

On the day itself, the Chancellor will begin his speech at just after 3.30 p.m. (The speech normally lasts about 75 to 90 minutes). He takes the opportunity to review the economic background against which the Budget has been prepared and goes on to tell his audience some of his expectations for the coming year.

The Chancellor then passes on to what most people regard as the interesting part of the Budget – the details of the tax changes he is planning to make.

The Government then publishes its *Financial Statement and Budget Report* giving details of the changes announced by the Chancellor, once he has finished his speech.

How the Budget Becomes Law

This is not the end of the matter by any means. The measures have to be made law and that means a *Bill* has to be passed by Parliament just like any other measure.

The Bill goes through a *Second Reading* debate, when all M.P.s have the chance to have their say about it. A *Finance Bill Committee* of about sixteen to twenty members is then appointed to examine the Bill clause by clause.

The Finance Bill Committee, having finished its work, reports back to the whole House and the Bill is then given its *Third Reading*. Unlike other Bills, the *Finance Bill* cannot be amended by the House of Lords, so it is now ready for the *Royal Assent*, to allow it to become law as the year's *Finance Act*. This usually occurs towards the end of July.

By the beginning of September thoughts are already turning to what might be in next year's Budget and the whole process begins again.

Further development

The following ideas could be used to develop this assignment.

1 Invite a local MP to talk about the role of the government.

2 Invite a speaker from your local authority to talk about its main sources of revenue and items of expenditure.

3 Study a nationalised industry and/or privatisation issue as a source of government revenue.

4 Examine the arguments *for* and *against* the proposed introduction of a community charge (poll tax) to replace the present system of rates.

Assignment 29

Safe and happy at work?

Introduction

Assignment 29 is an investigation into the health and safety aspects of a working environment. It can be undertaken as an individual or group exercise.

On completion of this assignment you should be able to:

1 explain how working conditions can affect a firm's efficiency;
2 identify potential health and safety hazards in your own 'working' environment;
3 describe potential health and safety hazards and how accidents can be prevented;
4 explain the effect on business activities of government regulations and legislation;
5 describe the main legal responsibilities of employers and employees with respect to health and safety.

Background information

Is your school or college a pleasant place in which to work? Is it too hot or cold? Is it draughty? Or is it brightly decorated, well lit and generally comfortable? How do you feel about it? We are all affected by the conditions in which we have to work. These physical conditions at work can affect everyone's health, safety and general welfare, which in turn can affect their efficiency and morale.

When we work efficiently we do things competently. That is, we do what is required accurately, quickly and well. However, a person's efficiency can be badly affected by poor working conditions. This may be due to inadequate lighting, heating, furniture and equipment, or due to too much noise or to a poor general layout of the work place. All of these factors can cause distractions, fatigue and strain.

Morale is the term used to describe the general atmosphere and spirit which affects a person's enthusiasm and behaviour at work. When morale is high, people feel happier at work and more confident in what they are doing. When morale is low people may lose interest in their work. This can reduce their efficiency and may result in a firm losing business. Morale is often affected by overcrowding at work, general discomfort or poor facilities, lack of communication and also poor management.

It is possible for good work to take place in poor working conditions, but usually, the better and safer the environment, then the more efficient a factory or office is likely to be.

Many firms recognise all these factors and take great care to ensure that staff are safe and happy at work. However, others do not, and therefore laws have been passed to protect people at work. One important law is the 1974 Health and Safety at Work Act which protects virtually all people at work.

The Act makes everyone concerned with work activities responsible for health and safety, including:

- employers, the self-employed, employees
- manufacturers, designers, suppliers and importers of articles and substances for use at work
- those in control of premises, for example, the Headteacher in a school.

The Act requires employers:

- to ensure that machinery and equipment are safely maintained and that work practices are safe;
- to provide safety training and produce a Safety Policy Statement of which all employees must be made aware.

Employees, for their part, are responsible for taking reasonable care at all times and for co-operating with the employer on safety matters.

Assignment

The following tasks are designed to develop your knowledge and understanding of the potential hazards in an organisation and what you can do to take responsibility for health and safety.

Tasks

1 Briefly explain the meaning of 'efficiency at work' and describe, using examples, three factors which can affect it. (5)
2 a Explain the meaning of 'morale'. (2)
  b Describe, with examples, the effects which 'low morale' can have on a business. (2)
3 From ABC's noticeboard overleaf identify the notices which relate to health and safety at work. (4)

TO ALL STAFF
Thursday next,
Canteen, 4.15 p.m.
UNION BRANCH MEETING
Agenda — REDUNDANCY
THREAT

VISITORS TO HEAD OFFICE:
Programme of visits by
the general public to the
offices and factory will
commence again next month

UNION ELECTIONS
Secretary, Shop Steward,
Health and Safety Representative.
You have a vote:
Make sure you use it.

Keep the work area
clean and tidy
at all times

HOLIDAY DATES:
The factory will close for 2 weeks
from 20 July — 2 August inclusive

FIRE ESCAPE/EXIT
→

NOTICE
It has come to my attention that certain members of the work force have been
in an unfit state for work after drinking in public houses during the lunch
break.

This practice must stop immediately.

J. Hall   Factory Manager

ABC's noticeboard

4 List *ten* potential health and safety hazards in this
   office.   (5)

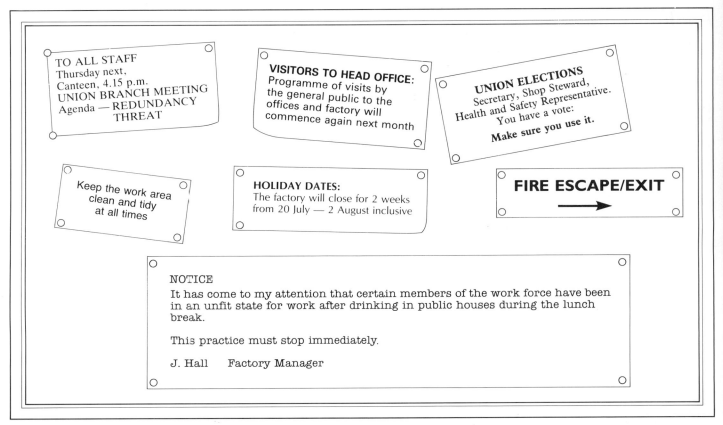

5 Briefly describe *five* of these hazards and suggest what could be done to help prevent accidents in this office. (5)

6 Recently a small office fire was caused by someone dropping a burning cigarette end into a wastepaper basket. Fortunately, on this occasion the fire was quickly spotted and little damage was done. Prepare an illustrated safety notice to warn all employees of the potential dangers of this practice. (5)

Lifting and carrying

There are good ways and bad ways of lifting things. The bad ways can hurt your back and your stomach. Ask your supervisor to show you the good ways to lift and move things. Don't lift things that are too big, too heavy, or too awkward for you to manage – ask for help. For some loads gloves and other special clothing should be worn.

Before you pick something up, be sure you know where it has to go, that the way there is clear and that you can put it down safely and securely when you get there. Whilst you are carrying it make sure you can see where you are going.

7 From the extract 'Lifting and carrying':
a identify the main risks involved when lifting objects; (2)

b give three basic rules which you should observe when lifting and carrying objects; (3)

c describe the correct method of lifting heavy and/or awkward objects safely. (2)

8 Explain what you should do if the fire alarm goes off in a building in which you are working/studying. (5)

9 Carry out a health and safety survey of your school/college/organisation making notes on potential hazards. Note the location of fire appliances, fire doors and fire exits and any relevant warning or direction notices. (5)

10 Describe what you think is your own responsibility for the health and safety of both yourself and the people with whom you attend school/college or work. (5)

Further development

The following ideas could be used to develop this assignment.

1 Examine the effects of new technology on the health and safety of employees. For example, what effect do visual display units have on people's health?

2 Arrange a talk by your organisation's safety officer/representative, or one from a local organisation.

3 Consider the risks to your health and safety when travelling to/from your school/college.

Assignment 30

But it's faulty

Introduction

Assignment 30 is a series of exercises on consumer protection. They can be completed as individual or group work, and some could be used for role play if desired.

On completion of this assignment you should be able to:

1 describe the aims and main features of consumer protection;
2 outline the main consumer protection legislation;
3 explain the activities of pressure groups protecting consumers;
4 appreciate the functions of voluntary codes and practices.

Background information

Most businesses are run honestly and deal with any problems which arise from the goods and services which they supply. Unfortunately, some traders are dishonest and they will often mislead consumers, sell faulty or dangerous products, give short weight or measure, or falsely describe goods in advertising or on labels. Therefore, some form of consumer protection is needed in these situations. This protection is provided through government legislation, consumer bodies and organisations, labelling and standards, and professional and trade associations.

Legislation

Sale of Goods Act 1979
This states that goods sold must be:

● **of merchantable quality**, considering the price and description. For example, whilst a pair of shoes costing £35 would be expected to wear better than a pair costing £10.99, if you bought a new pair of shoes you would not expect the heel to come off soon after you started wearing them.
● **as described.** Thus plastic shoes should not be called leather.
● **fit for the purpose** for which they are generally used. If glue is sold to mend shoes then it must do just that.

If any of these conditions is not met, then customers are entitled to return goods and receive compensation in the form of a full or part cash refund, repair or exchange. The shop is responsible for the goods it sells.

Trade Descriptions Acts 1968 and 1972
These Acts make it an offence for traders to falsely describe goods and services.

● Descriptions like 'made of wool', 'low fat', or 'made in Britain' must be true.
● Goods must only be marked as reduced if they have been selling at a higher price for at least 28 consecutive days during the previous six months. If not this must be made clear, for example, 'last week's price £1.99, now £1.25.

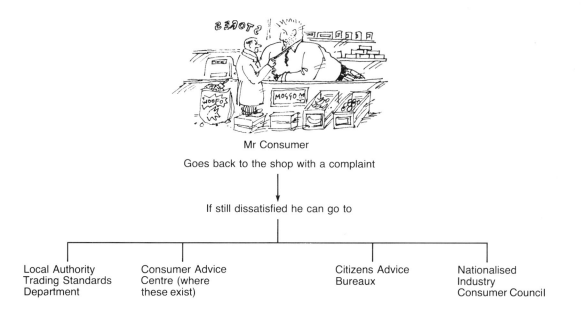

Mr Consumer

Goes back to the shop with a complaint

↓

If still dissatisfied he can go to

| Local Authority Trading Standards Department | Consumer Advice Centre (where these exist) | Citizens Advice Bureaux | Nationalised Industry Consumer Council |

Consumer complaints

Fair Trading Act 1973

This set up the **Office of Fair Trading (OFT)** to look after consumer affairs and consumer credit. The OFT publishes information leaflets, prosecutes offenders, issues credit licences, encourages competition and fair trading, and recommends new laws.

Consumer Credit Act 1974

This protects consumers in most transactions involving up to £5,000 of credit. Its main provisions include:

- all credit traders must be licenced by the OFT.
- borrowers must be advised of the true cost of interest on any loan. This is known as the annual percentage rate (APR).
- consumers are allowed a 'cooling-off' period of 5 days in which to change their mind and cancel any credit agreement which is signed off trade premises, for example, at home.

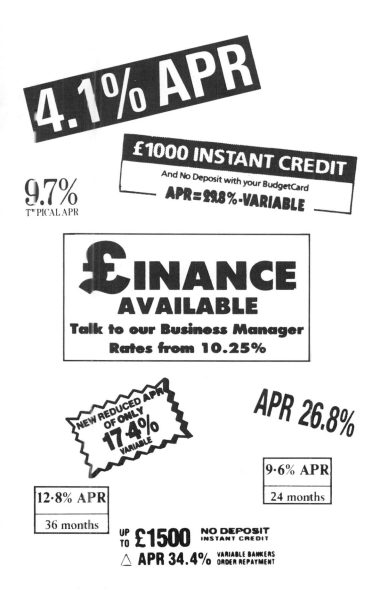

The cost of credit

Consumer Safety Act 1986

This aims to prevent the sale of dangerous goods.

Food and Drugs Acts 1955, 1976 and 1982

These Acts are concerned with the hygiene, composition and labelling of food and make it an offence to sell food which is unfit to eat.

Weights and Measures Act 1985

This Act makes it an offence for traders to give short weight or measure. Inspectors visit trade premises such as shops, public houses and garages to check that the scales, beer or petrol pumps used are accurate.

Unsolicited Goods and Services Act 1971

This Act makes it an offence for a trader to demand payment for goods sent through the post which people have not ordered.

Consumer bodies and organisations

The OFT itself cannot take up individual consumer complaints about unfair trading practices. Instead it provides information and advice for consumers and issues many leaflets. Most are available free from local authority Trading Standards Departments, Consumer Advice Centres, Citizens Advice Bureaux (CAB), Nationalised Industry Consumer Councils and other organisations which help to enforce the consumer protection laws.

Labelling and standards

Consumers can also help to protect themselves by buying goods which carry recognised safety standard labels including the British Standards Institution (BSI) kitemark, the Gas Council kitemark or the Design Council label. These are independent organisations which test products for quality and safety.

The **Consumers Association** also aims to help consumers by testing products and comparing them. Reports are published in its monthly magazine, *Which?*, thereby helping consumers to choose the best buy.

Professional and Trade Associations

These are formed when firms in the same industry join together to protect their interests and deal with common problems, for example, ABTA (Association of British Travel Agents), ASA (Advertising Standards Authority) and MAA (Motor Agents Association). The OFT encourages these various associations to draw up voluntary Codes of Practice aimed at improving the standards of goods and services.

Nowadays then, any consumer with a genuine complaint should be able to get things put right. From a retailer's point of view it is better to have a satisfied customer than to lose custom and gain a bad reputation.

Holiday and Travel

Motor Cars

Hotels and Catering

Shoe Repairs

All these trade associations have easily identifable logos

Assignment

You are asked to complete the following tasks which are designed to develop your knowledge and understanding of consumer protection in Britain today.

Tasks

1 State which law is being broken in each of the following situations:
   a A company demands payment for a book sent through the post but not ordered by the customer.
   b A jacket which the salesman claimed was made of leather was in fact made of plastic.
   c A customer purchases 5 lb of potatoes but on weighing them at home finds she has only received 4 lb 4 ozs.
   d A customer buys a rainproof coat which fails to keep him dry.
   e You agree to buy double glazing on credit from a salesman who calls at your home, but the company refuses to let you cancel the agreement the following day. (5)

2 Briefly explain the following terms and give one example of each:
   a Independent organisation
   b Trade association
   c Professional association
   d Code of practice
   e Safety standards. (10)

3 Write out in full the name of the organisation known by the following abbreviations. Some are mentioned in the background information.
   a ABTA   f CA
   b ASA   g IBA
   c BSI   h MOPS
   d CAB   i OFT
   e CAC   j POUNC (5)

4 From Task 3 select the most appropriate organisation/ body which could offer help and advice in each of the following situations.
   a You order a lawn mower through the classified advertising section of a national Sunday newspaper. After waiting two months the company has still not delivered it, and you fear that it may have gone bankrupt.
   b You have strong views on proposed increases in postal charges and you wish to make a protest.
   c An advertisement in your local newspaper makes a statement which you are certain is untrue.
   d Your holiday hotel in Majorca is not the one which you selected from the company's brochure.
   e You plan to purchase a new washing machine and would like to read an independent report on the most suitable type before making a decision. (5)

5 Victor Pedlingham owns a sports shop in which he sells a wide range of clothing and equipment. He does not offer credit facilities to his customers but accepts the most common credit cards. He buys most of his stock from Barnett's – a local manufacturer.

   Chris Wright, a well-known athlete, recently went into the shop to buy a pair of running shoes and a tracksuit. He particularly requested a pair of shoes which he could use for training, much of which he did on hard surfaces. Chris purchased both items using his Visa card.

   The tracksuit was satisfactory, but after just three training sessions the shoes showed considerable signs of wear on the heels and the soles were beginning to come away from the uppers. Chris could not find his receipt but nonetheless he returned to the shop and complained to Victor who was unhappy that there was no proof of purchase. However, Victor said that the problem was due to the shoes being used on an unsuitable surface and unfortunately there was nothing he could do about it.

   In any case, he stated, it was not really his responsibility since he had purchased the shoes from the manufacturer and if Mr Wright had a complaint he must take it to Barnett's.
   a Is Victor Pedlingham correct in what he says? Explain your answer. (5)
   b What rights has Chris Wright? (6)
   c What should Barnett's do about the situation? (4)
   d Name two organisations which could help Chris with his complaint. (2)
   e Advise Chris on the course of action he should take to enforce his rights. (8)

Further development

The following ideas could be used to develop this
assignment

1 Invite a speaker from your local Trading Standards
  Department, Consumer Advice Centre or Citizens
  Advice Bureau to talk about consumers' rights.
2 Using issues of *Which?*, make a study of the role of the
  Consumers Association. These should be available in the
  library.
3 Examine the functions of the Office of Fair Trading.

H

Multiple choice 5

This section contains a series of questions or incomplete sentences followed by four possible responses. In each case select the most appropriate answer.

1 Which of the following could be considered as a social benefit arising from a new industrial development in an area?
   a Increased traffic congestion
   b Air pollution
   c Creation of more jobs
   d Need for more schools

2 Which of the following measures would *not* be used by the government to encourage industry to move to assisted areas?
   a Investment allowances
   b Improved transport facilities
   c Providing ready-built factories
   d Higher taxation

3 Which of the following regions suffers from the highest rate of unemployment?
   a Northern Ireland
   b South East England
   c East Anglia
   d Yorkshire and Humberside

4 The organisation set up by the government to help improve industrial relations is called:
   a TUC
   b CBI
   c BSI
   d ACAS.

5 Girobank is run by the:
   a Post Office
   b Treasury
   c Bank of England
   d Merchant banks.

6 Which of the following is an example of an indirect tax?
   a Income tax
   b Corporation tax
   c Capital gains tax
   d Value added tax

7 Income tax is a progressive tax. This means that:
   a it increases every year;
   b it is a fixed percentage regardless of income;
   c the higher a person's income the greater the percentage of tax deducted;
   d it represents all the money spent by the government.

8 Which of the following is *not* a source of revenue for local authorities?
   a Income from trading activities
   b Value added tax
   c Grants from central government
   d Income from rent and rates

9 Which of the following is an item of local rather than central government expenditure?
   a Social Services
   b Social Security
   c National Health Service
   d Defence

10 If a house has a rateable value of £500 and the local authority rate is 90p in the £, the owner will pay:
   a £50
   b £410
   c £450
   d £500

11 During a period of inflation which of the following is least likely to suffer:
   a the unemployed
   b people on fixed incomes
   c members of a strong trade union
   d pensioners.

12 The Bank of England may use all except which *one* of the following measures to control the economy?
   a Open market operations
   b Fiscal policies
   c Official lending rates
   d Controls on bank lending

13 Which of the following laws was *not* introduced with the aim of protecting employees and improving their conditions of employment?
   a Contract of Employment Act 1972
   b Health and Safety At Work Act 1974
   c Sex Discrimination Act 1975
   d Unfair Contract Terms Act 1977

14 Which of the following statements about the Health and Safety at Work Act 1974 is incorrect?
   a It set up a Health and Safety Commission.
   b It introduced improvement and prohibition orders.
   c It does not apply to self-employed workers.
   d It requires employers to produce a safety policy.

15 The functions of the Office of Fair Trading do *not* include:
   a dealing directly with consumer complaints;
   b publishing information leaflets for consumers;
   c prosecuting traders who persistently commit offences;
   d licensing credit traders.

16 A consumer who receives a demand for the payment of goods which have *not* been ordered is protected by the:
   a Trade Descriptions Act 1968
   b Unsolicited Goods and Services Act 1971
   c Sale of Goods Act 1979
   d Fair Trading Act 1968.

17 The Motor Agents Association is an example of a:
   a Trade union
   b Trade association
   c Government department
   d Public limited company.

In each of the following questions, one or more of the responses is/are correct. Choose the appropriate letter which indicates the correct version.
   a If 1 only is correct.
   b If 3 only is correct.
   c If 1 and 2 only are correct.
   d If 1, 2 and 3 are correct.

18 Which of the following organisations offer protection to consumers against misleading or offensive advertising?
   1 Advertising Standards Authority
   2 Mail Order Protection Society
   3 Confederation of British Industry

19 Which of the following is/are a form of government borrowing?
   1 Treasury bills
   2 National savings
   3 Customs duties

20 Which of the following is/are the main economic aims of the government?
   1 To control inflation
   2 To increase economic growth
   3 To redistribute income and wealth

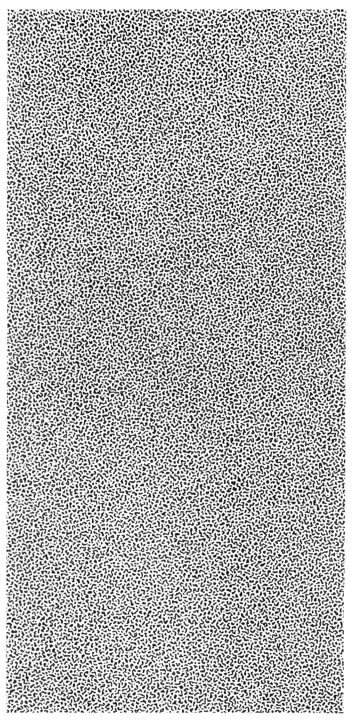

Revision

Introduction

Assignment 31 is a problem solving exercise based on two young people setting up their own business. It can be carried out in groups or individually. You will need to use knowledge which you have gained throughout your GCSE Business Studies course. Therefore, for some tasks you may find it helpful to use the glossary and refer to the background information given in other assignments. A dictionary, Thomson's Local Telephone Directory and Yellow Pages will be useful for reference.

On completion of this assignment you should be able to:

1 recognise the major objectives of a business;
2 appreciate how a business can identify its markets;
3 explain the issues associated with setting up in business;
4 apply your knowledge from previous assignments.

Sharon and Tracy at work

Assignment

Read the situation below and complete the tasks that follow.

Sharon Evans and Tracy Lewis are both 18. Since leaving school they have had a number of part-time jobs in the catering trade but so far have not managed to find full-time employment. For the past six months they have been unemployed. After watching a recent television programme on healthy eating they had an idea for starting their own business.

Their idea was to produce a small range of quality vegetarian convenience foods, prepared using only fresh vegetables. This could be started from home with the minimum of capital investment. They had thought of selling the products in returnable crock pots to the catering trade and in microwave proof containers for home consumption.

After carrying out some small scale research they were convinced that there was a local market for the products. However, not knowing very much about business studies they ask you for some written advice about the problems which they may face and what they need to do to get started.

Tasks

1 Propose what might be suitable objectives for the business in its first year of trading. *(3)*
2 Suggest three sources of market research information which could be used to find out about the potential market. *(3)*
3 a Define what is meant by 'the catering trade'. *(2)*
  b Identify eight potential outlets in your area for the girls' products. *(4)*
4 Describe what is meant by convenience foods and suggest four local competitors. *(4)*
5 a Describe the capital investment which will be needed to start the business. *(4)*
  b Suggest three sources of finance which could be used. *(3)*
6 List and describe at least five major issues which the girls must resolve before starting up their business. *(10)*
7 List the likely overheads which must be covered. *(3)*
8 Identify five agencies/organisations which help people to set up or run their own business. *(5)*
9 Suggest a suitable brand name for the product range and describe four promotional methods which could be used to launch the business. *(5)*
10 Recommend, with reasons, an appropriate legal structure for the business. *(4)*

Further development

The following ideas could be used to develop this assignment.

1 A sales forecast and break-even chart could be prepared.
2 A speaker could be invited from the Small Firms Information Centre and/or the catering trade to talk about setting up a business.
3 The problems associated with the seasonal availability of fresh supplies and resultant variations in cost could be investigated.
4 The problems associated with pricing could be examined. Some research into the average cost of vegetarian meals might be useful as would a look at the likely effect of different prices on demand for the girls' products.
5 Prepare a complete business plan for submission to a bank.

Assignment 32

Introduction

Assignment 32 is a crossword designed for revision purposes. You will need to use knowledge which you have gained throughout your Business Studies course. It can be carried out as an individual or group exercise.

If you have problems then use the glossary or Index to help you or refer back to your earlier assignment work.

Assignment

Solve the crossword below using the clues provided. (40)

Let's revise

Across

1 Division of ...... (6)
3 Exchange of goods (6)
7 Current asset (4)
8 Used for new products (4)
10 Indirect tax (3)
11 Determines insurance premium (4)
13 Method of transport (4)
15 Type of profit (3)
18 Order by post (4)
19 Limited liability (3)
21 Income tax (4)
23 Written on a 'bounced' cheque (2)
24 Used 'in' a dispute (3)
26 Stock Exchange 'baby' (3)
28 Borrowed money (4)
30 Market research agency (3)
31 Chart presentation (3)
32 Abbreviation for sales (2)
34 See 26 Down
35 Government training scheme for school-leavers (3)
36 Abbreviation, can be, trade or cash (3)

Down

1 Form of integration (7)
2 Consumer protection body (3)
3 Giro.... (4)
4 AC.. provides assistance in industrial disputes (2)
5 Hire pu.c.ase (2)
6 Link in chain of distribution (6)
9 Four 'P's in the marketing ... (3)
12 Internal communication (4)
14 Bank statement abbreviation (2)
16 Gross Profit Account abbreviated (2)
17 Savings account (6)
20 Countries do this with surplus goods (4)
21 Business objective (6)
22 ..vertising (2)
25 Government revenue (5)
26 and 34 Across Form of investment (4,5)
27 Bank statement abbreviation (2)
29 White collar union (3)
31 Sometimes added to a letter (2)
33 'In the red' at bank abbreviation (2)

Glossary of business terms

Arbitration: settlement of an industrial dispute by an independent person or body

Articles of Association: set of rules which regulate the internal management of a company including voting rights and how profits are shared

Authority: power given by managers to subordinates to enable them to carry out instructions

Automation: use of machinery to replace labour in performing industrial and administrative processes and operations

Bank draft: cheque drawn on a bank

Bank Giro: method used by clearing banks to transfer money rapidly from one account to another

Bankrupt: person or business unable to meet its debts

Bank statement: written statement from a bank giving details of credits, debits and balance of an account

Basic pay: minimum amount of pay for a normal working week

Bill of Exchange: document which tells a bank to pay a person, mainly used for foreign trade payments

Bill of Lading: 'document of title' used when goods are transported by sea; it gives details of cargo and provides proof of ownership

Birth rate: number of births per thousand of the population

Bonus: extra sum of money paid to employees as a reward for hard work or improved efficiency

'Bounced' cheque: cheque on which the bank refuses payment because there is insufficient money in the account to cover it

Branch: local part of a trade union to which members belong

Budget: plan of expected income and expenditure, usually over one year

Budget account: bank account into which a set amount is paid each month. Payments are made to meet expenses as they arise

Capital: value of assets (wealth) owned by a business and used to create further capital. May include money, machinery, stock and premises

   Authorised: total amount of money that a limited company may obtain by issuing shares

   Issued: the value of shares actually issued to shareholders in return for cash

Cash discount: percentage deduction from the price of goods or services to encourage prompt payment

Certificate of Incorporation: issued by Registrar of Companies to new company, which meets the legal requirements, allowing it to begin trading

Cheque: written instruction to a bank asking them to pay a certain amount of money to someone else

Closed shop: where all employees in a firm must be members of a trade union

Codes of Practice: rules drawn up by an association which members agree to follow in the course of their business

Communication: process of passing information from one person to another

Community charge (poll tax): local tax to replace rates

Confravision: telecommunication service which links different places by sound and vision

Consequential loss: additional financial loss resulting from an insured risk, e.g. extra expense following a fire

Consumer: individual or organisation which purchases goods and/or services

Contract: legal agreement used in business between two or more people stating the terms of a transaction

Contribution: if a risk is insured with more than one insurance company then any loss would be shared between them, i.e. each would contribute

Conurbation: continuous built-up area linking several towns or cities, e.g. Greater London

Credit: being allowed to pay for goods or services over a period of time

Credit card: plastic card which allows goods to be purchased without immediate payment

Creditor: someone to whom a business owes money, e.g. a supplier of stock who has not been paid

Current account: bank account used for day-to-day transactions

Death rate: number of deaths per thousand of the population

Debentures: long-term loan stock issued by companies to raise capital. Debentures usually carry a fixed rate of interest and guaranteed repayment at a future date

Debtor: someone who owes money to a business, e.g. for goods which they have bought

Delegation: term used to describe instructions given by managers to their subordinates

Demand: the amount of goods or services which consumers are willing to buy, at a given price, over a period of time, e.g. 400 units @ £5 each per week

Deposit account: bank account used for savings on which interest is paid

Depreciation: amount by which assets lose their value over a period of time

Direct debit: when a customer instructs their bank to allow a payee to withdraw money from their account, often used for regular payments

Direct tax: tax which is paid directly to the government, e.g. income tax

Director: person appointed by shareholders to help run a company on their behalf

Diseconomies of scale: reduced efficiency and rising costs per unit resulting from a firm growing too large

Disintegration: individual firms specialising in one part of the production process

Drawee: the name of the bank on which a cheque is drawn

Drawer: person who writes and signs a cheque

Dumping: term used to refer to 'surplus' foreign goods which are sold ('dumped') abroad at a lower price than in the home market. This creates unfair competition

E and O E (Errors and Omissions Excepted): this is shown on many invoices and enables firms to correct any mistakes

Earnings: payments received in the form of wages or salaries, profits, dividends or interest

Economic growth: annual increase in the national income

Economies of scale: advantages gained from operating on a larger scale, e.g. by producing goods in larger quantities

Endowment policy: a life policy which pays out benefit on an agreed date or on death, if earlier

Entrepreneur: someone who brings together the factors of production (land, labour, capital) and organises them into a 'business', taking risks in anticipation of making a profit

Ex-works: factory price of goods excluding the cost of transport and delivery

Facsimile: an exact copy of a letter or document

Factoring: buying of business debts at a discount

Factors of production: essential resources needed for production, consisting of land, labour, capital and enterprise

Fiscal policy: government policies based on the use of taxation and public expenditure

Franchise company: a company which sets people up in business and allows them to use its name and products in return for a fee

Free trade: trade between countries free of any tariffs, quotas or other protective measures

'Futures' market: trading situation where a price is agreed now for goods which will be delivered at some future date, perhaps in three or six months time. Foreign exchange is frequently bought in this way, as are sugar, grains and metals.

Goods: physical items which can be purchased, e.g. houses, furniture, soap powder, stationery

Hire purchase: purchasing of goods on credit. Payments are made by regular instalments, e.g. £20 per month for two years.

Hypermarket: very large supermarket located on the outskirts of large towns or cities

Impulse buying: unplanned spending, goods bought on the spur of the moment

Indirect tax: tax which is not collected directly by the government, e.g. VAT

Industrial relations: relations between management and its employees

'Infant' industries: young (or new) industries which may need protection from foreign competition to enable them to develop and grow

Inflation: situation where prices are generally rising

Integration: where businesses join together as a result of a takeover or merger

Interest: charge made for the use of borrowed money

Investment: money used to earn a financial return, e.g. buying shares

Job description: outline of main duties and responsibilities of a job

Job satisfaction: combination of factors which motivate people and help them to enjoy their work

Labour: skills and efforts of people used to convert land into goods and services

Land: all the natural resources used by man, e.g. soil, coal, trees and fish

Leasing: hiring or renting of assets rather than buying outright

Life expectancy: average number of years a person can expect to live

Limited liability: should a business fail, investors cannot lose any of their personal possessions, i.e. liability is limited to the amount invested

Loan: sum of money lent for a period of time. Interest is charged on the amount borrowed.

Market: any situation where buyers and sellers come into contact

Market share: value of a firm's sales as a proportion of the total sales in a market

Marketing mix: the four 'P's of product, price, promotion and place which together make up a marketing plan for a business

Mark-up: amount added to the cost price of an item to arrive at its selling price

Mass media: means of communication designed to reach large numbers of people, e.g. television, newspapers

Mass production: manufacturing of goods in large quantities

Media: different means of communication, e.g. advertising, telephone, letters

Memorandum of Association: document giving details of the rules governing the external affairs of a company including its name, address, objectives and capital

Merger: joining together of two or more companies

Microfilming: taking miniature photographs of data to make it easier to store (file)

Monetary policy: government's financial policy based on control of interest rates and bank lending

Morale: general emotional feeling of a group or individual, e.g. enthusiasm or loyalty

Mortgage: loan for the purchase of property

Motivation: factors which encourage or discourage people at work, often linked with job satisfaction

National debt: amount owed by the government of a country

National income: total annual output, in money terms, of all goods and services produced in a country

Night safe: safe found on outside wall of banks which enables deposit of money and documents when bank is closed

Objectives: what a business aims to achieve, e.g. profit, growth, market share

Optimum population: level of population at which income per head is at its maximum

Overdraft: being allowed to take more money out of a bank current account than there is in it, i.e. to overdraw

Overheads: expenses of running a business – e.g. advertising, rent, wages – whatever its sales or production

Overtime: time spent at work in excess of normal working day or week for which additional money is usually paid

Payee: person to whom a certain sum of money is to be paid

Poll tax (community charge): standard charge on everyone in a household over the age of 18. Local tax to replace rates

Prestel: two-way communication system which provides a data base of information via a specially adapted television set

Primary production: the first stage of production involving extractive industries, e.g. agriculture, forestry, mining

Privatisation: government policy of selling off public corporations to the private sector as public limited companies, e.g. British Telecom, British Gas

Production: making or manufacturing of goods for sale

Productivity agreement: wage increases related directly to increases in output

Profit: money left over after expenses have been paid
  Gross: profit made from sales of goods or services before deduction of overheads
  Net: profit after deduction of all expenses

Rates: set and collected by local authorities to help meet their expenditure. Every type of property is given a rateable value on which rates at a fixed amount in the £ must be paid. (*see also* **Poll Tax**)

Reserves: savings, profits or other money retained for future use

Responsibility: when a manager can delegate a task but is still ultimately accountable for the work carried out

Retail Price Index (RPI): used to measure changes in the value of money

Ring trading: this is used, for example, on the London Metal Exchange. The dealers gather in a circle and shout out the price at which they are prepared to buy or sell a particular metal until a price is agreed.

Sample: used in market research to ask a representative group of people what they think about a product or service

Secondary production: the manufacturing or construction stage of production, e.g. engineering, building

Share: capital which represents part ownership of a company

Shareholder: a person who owns shares in a company

Shop steward: union member elected to represent others in their place of work

Social costs: ways in which a business decision will affect a local community

'Spot' Trading: trading situation where goods are sold at a cash price for immediate delivery. Examples might include tea, coffee and oil

Standing order: written instruction by a customer to a bank to make regular payments on their behalf

Stock Exchange: market where second-hand shares are bought and sold

Stockturn: number of times average stock is sold during a trading period

Superannuation: amount deducted from employees wages to pay for a pension on retirement

Supply: the amount of goods or services which businesses are willing to offer for sale, at a given price over a period of time, e.g. 200 units per week @ £2 each

Takeover: buying of one company by another

Technology: application of scientific processes to improve production and efficiency, e.g. computers and robots

Tertiary production: distribution stage of production which also includes other service industries, e.g. transport, banking, insurance

Trade association: group of companies in a similar trade or profession

Trade credit: when a trader sells goods to another trader and allows time for payment

Trade discount: percentage reduction in price given to businesses in the same trade

Trade price: price at which goods are bought by businesses

Turnover: accounting term for the total sales of a business over a period of time, e.g. one year

Unlisted Securities Market (USM): known as 'second-tier' stock market and often used by young companies going public (i.e. offering their shares for sale to the public for the first time)

Value added tax (VAT): tax on goods and services

Wealth: the quantity of money or assets possessed

Yield: calculation to show the annual percentage return on capital

A list of useful addresses

ACAS
11 – 12 St James's Square
LONDON
SW1Y 4LA

Access
Priory Crescent
SOUTHEND-ON-SEA
SS2 6QQ

Advertising Standards Authority
Brook House
2 – 16 Torrington Place
LONDON
WC1E 7HN

Bank Education Service
10 Lombard Street
LONDON
EC3V 9AT

Bank of England
Threadneedle Street
LONDON
EC2R 8AH

Barclaycard
NORTHAMPTON
NN1 1YU

Board of Customs and Excise
King's Beam House
Mark Lane
LONDON
EC3R 3HE

Board of Trade
1 Victoria Street
LONDON SW1

British Electro-Technical Approvals Board (BEAB)
153 London Road
KINGSTON-UPON-THAMES
Surrey
KT12 5NA

British Gas plc
152 Grosvenor Road
LONDON
SW1V 3JL

British Insurance Brokers Association
10 Bevis Marks
LONDON
EC3

British Overseas Trade Board
1 Victoria Street
LONDON
SW1H 0ET

British Standards Institution
2 Park Street
LONDON
W1A 2BS

British Telecommunications plc
81 Newgate Street
LONDON
EC1A 7AJ

British Tourist Authority
Thames Tower
Blacks Road
LONDON
W6 9EL

Building Societies Association
14 Park Street
LONDON
W1X 4AL

Central Office of Information
Hercules Road
LONDON
SE1 7DU

Central Statistical Office
Great George Street
LONDON
SW1P 3AQ

Confederation of British Industry
Centre Point
103 New Oxford Street
LONDON
WC1A 1DU

Consumers Association (*WHICH?*)
14 Buckingham Street
LONDON
WC2N 6DS

Department of Employment
Caxton House
Tothill Street
LONDON
SW1H 9NF

Department of National Savings
375 Kensington High Street
LONDON
W14 8SD

Department of Trade and Industry
1 Victoria Street
LONDON
SW1H OET

Design Centre
28 Haymarket
LONDON
SW1Y 4 SU

European Commission
8 Storey's Gate
LONDON
SW1P 3AT

Good Housekeeping Institute
Vauxhall Bridge Road
LONDON
SW1V 1HF

HMSO
St Crispins
Duke Street
NORWICH
NR3 1PD

Independent Broadcasting Authority
70 Brompton Road
LONDON
SW3 1EY

Inland Revenue Press and Information Officer
New Wing
Somerset House
Strand
LONDON
WC2R 1LB

Lord's Day Observance Society
5 Victory Avenue
MORDEN
Surrey
SM4 6DL

Market Research Society
15 Belgrave Square
LONDON
SW1X 8PF

National Chamber of Trade
Enterprise House
HENLEY-ON-THAMES
Oxon
RG9 1TU

Northern Ireland Dept of Economic Development
176 Newtownbreda Road
BELFAST
BT8 4QS

Office of Fair Trading
Bromyard Avenue
Acton
LONDON
W3 7BB

Port of London Authority
Leslie Ford House
Tilbury Docks
Essex
RM18 7EH

Schools' Officer
Postal Headquarters
St Martins-le-Grand
LONDON
EC1A 1HQ

The Stock Exchange Information Office
Throgmorton Street
LONDON
EC2 1HP

Trades Union Congress
Great Russell Street
LONDON
WC1B 3LS

Training Commission
Moorfoot
SHEFFIELD
S1 4PQ

USDAW
188 Wilmslow Road
MANCHESTER
M14 6LJ

Index

This index is based on the Background Information only and the reference given refers to the Assignment number. Terms not fully explained in the text are included in the glossary.

ACAS 22
Account 5
  Budget
  Current
  Deposit
Accounts 5, 20
  Bank 5
  Final 20
Advertising 16
  Agencies
  Control of
  Cost of
  Media
  Standards Authority
Age distribution 2
Assets 3, 20
  External 3
  Fixed and current 20
Assisted Areas 27
Assurance 13
Average costs 11, 19

Balance of Payments 3
Balance of Trade 3
Balance on Current Account 3
Balancing Item 3
Banking 5, 6
Barter *Introduction*
Bills of Exchange 5
Board of Directors 8
Branded goods 16
Break-even point/chart 19
Broker/dealer 12
Budget, The 28
Budget account 5
Building societies 5
Business departments 21
Business documents 18
Business finance 12
Business organisation 7

Capital 12, 20
  Return on 20
  Working 20
Cash discount 18
Cashless Society 6
Chain of distribution 9
Chain stores 9
Cheques 5, 6
Choice 7
Citizens Advice Bureaux 30
Collective bargaining 22
Communications 11, 24
Companies
  Private 7, 12
  Public 7, 12

Computer services 8
Conglomerates 11
Consumer 30
  Advice Centres
  Association
  Credit Act
  Protection
  Safety Act
Containers 17
Controlled economy 7
Conurbations 2
Co-operatives 7, 9
CWS 9
Cost-benefit analysis 25
Costs 11, 19
  Average 11, 19
  Fixed 19
  Variable 19
Credit cards 6
Credit note 18
Current account 5
Customs union 4

Debit note 18
Demand 8, 12
Department stores 9
Deposit account 5
Direct debit 5, 6
Discount stores 9
Diseconomies of scale 11
Disintegration 11
Division of labour *Introduction*, 1
Documents, business 18
Door to door selling 9
Drawee 5
Drawer 5
Dumping 3

EFTPOS 6
Economic systems 7
Economies of scale 3, 11
Efficiency 11, 21, 29
Embargoes 3
European Community 4
Exchange control 3
Exports 3

Factoring 5
Fair Trading Act 30
Finance 8, 12
Fixed costs 19
Food and Drugs Acts 30
Franchising 7
Fringe benefits 23
Free markets 7

Girobank 27
Government
  Business organisation 7
  Departments 7
  International trade 3
  Legislation 30
  Location of industry 10
  Revenue/expenditure 28
  Sunday trading 26
  Unemployment 28

Health and safety at work 29
Hire purchase 12
Holding companies 11
Hypermarkets 9, 10

Imports 3
Income tax 23, 28
Industrial action 22
Industrial relations 11, 21
Insurance 13
  Business insurance
  Documents
  Premiums
  Principles of
Integration 11
  Horizontal
  Lateral
  Vertical
Interest 5
International trade 3
Invisible trade 3
Invoice 18

Job satisfaction 21

Leasing 12
Liabilities 3, 20
  External 3
  Fixed and current 20
Limited liability 7, 12
Line management 8
Loans 3, 5, 12
Local authority 7
Location of industry 10

Mail order 9
Management 8
  Line
  Staff
Market-makers 12
Marketing 8, 14, 15
  Mix 14
Market research 14
Markets 9, 10
Mixed economy 7

Mobile Shops 9
MOPS 16
Morale 29
Multi-national companies 11
Multiple stores 9
Municipal undertakings 7

Nationalisation 7
Nationalised industry consumer councils 30
New towns 27
Night safe 5

Objectives 8
Office of Fair Trading 30
Order 18
Overdraft 5, 12

Partnerships 7, 12
Party selling 9
Pay 23
    Deductions from
PAYE 23
Payee 5
Personnel 8
    Functions of 21
Population 2
    Birth rate
    Census
    Death rate
    Geographical distribution
    Life expectancy
    Migration
    Occupational distribution
    Working population
Post Office 5
Primary industry 2, 10
Production *Introduction*, 1, 8
Product life cycle 15
Profit 8, 19, 20
    Gross 20
    Net 20
Protection 3
Private sector 7, 8

Public corporations 7, 8
Public sector 7, 8

Questionnaire 14
Quotas 3

Reserves 3
Retail trade 9
    Types of

Salaries 23
Sale of Goods Act 30
Sales promotion 16
Sampling 14
Scale of production 11
Scarcity 7
Secondary industry 2, 10
Self-sufficiency *Introduction*, 3
Self-service stores 9
Shareholders 12
Shops (*see* Retail trade)
Shops Act 26
Social costs and benefits 25
Sole proprietor 7, 9, 12
Specialisation 1, 3
Standing order 5, 6
Statement 18
    Bank 5
    Business document 18
    Credit card 6
Stock average 20
Stock Exchange 12
Strikes 22
Subsidies 3
Sunday trading 26
Supermarkets 9
Supply 8, 12

Tariffs 3
Taxation 28
Technology 6, 27
    Computer 6

Tertiary industry 2, 10
Trade *Introduction*, 3
    Free 3, 4
    Discount 18
    International 3
Trade Description Acts 30
Trade fairs/exhibitions 9
Trade union 22
Trading and profit loss account
    (*see* Accounts, Final)
Trading Standards Department 30
Training commission 27
Transport 17
    Future development
    Importance of
    Types of
Turnover 19, 20
    Profit on 20
    Rate of 20

Unemployment 2, 3, 27
Unsolicited Goods and Services
    Act 30

VAT 18, 28
Variable costs 19
Vending machines 9
Visible trade 3

Wages 23
    Gross
    Net
Weights and Measures Act 30
Wholesalers 9
    Functions of
    Future of
    Types of
Working conditions 29
Work to rule 22

Yield 20

Acknowledgements

We are grateful to the following for permission to reproduce copyright material which is indicated by the assignment number.

Advertising Standards Authority 16
Banking Information Service 5
BP Oil Ltd 17
Cadbury-Schweppes (and their Advertising Agents Saatchi and Saatchi) 15
Caroline Horrigan 14, 29
Crown Copyright 2
European Parliament 4
Freightliners Ltd 17
Godfrey Hill 24
Mail Order Protection Scheme 16
Manpower Services Commission 29
Observer 6
J Sainsbury plc. 9
Stock Exchange 28

Photographs are reproduced with the permission of the following:
Chris Davies, Network, p.10; European Parliament, p.17; Liz Somerville, pp.20, 41, 58, 91; *Financial Times*, p.23; J Sainsbury plc., p.34; Bob Watkins, p.51; British Petroleum, p.59; Derek Pratt, p.60; Raissa Page, Format, p.62; Inda Passow, Network, p.68; Martin Jenkinson, N.U.J., p.76; Brenda Prince, Format, p.88; John Sturrock, Network, p.94.

The authors also wish to thank all the companies and newspapers for the use of other material. (Despite every effort, we have failed to trace the copyright holders for some of the illustrations.)

We are also indebted to Godfrey Hill and Chris Winter who made a major contribution to the planning of this text and participated in classroom evaluation.

Finally to our families without whose help, encouragement and tolerance, the book would not have been possible.

S.D.
L.C.